CAIRNGORM

GLENS

THE CAIRNGORM GLENS

A personal survey of the Cairngorm Glens
for mountainbikers and walkers

by

Peter D. Koch-Osborne

CICERONE PRESS, MILNTHORPE, CUMBRIA

© P.D. Koch-Osborne 1991
ISBN 1 85284 086 2

Wheresoever you go, remain a hermit
   inwardly, then your world can
   never weaken you.
Do not leave your peace where you found it
Bring it back with you into this life, whose
   agitation can then rarely reach you.
Hold to it as your most treasured possession,
   and, unafraid, you may let all storms
   blow past you.

                                        anon.

Index

Introduction

Access to the tracks and paths depicted on the following pages can never be regarded as an absolute 'right' by the cyclist or walker. All land is privately owned and it is only the good nature of the landowner that allows us to travel unhindered over his land. In law no such term as trespass exists in Scotland, nuisance or damage has to be proven in order to eject persons from the land but in practice sensible conduct is all that is required to maintain free access. Respect the grouse and deer stalking seasons whatever your views on the subject of "blood" sports. The author has never met with any animosity in meetings with estate workers. Your conduct will keep it this way.

Conservation of the unique wildness of the Cairngorm region is of paramount importance. Much has been written elsewhere but for the purposes of users of this guidebook it must be appreciated that the very ground over which you walk or cycle will be damaged if care is not taken. Please don't use a bike on soft peat paths, tread carefully when walking on other than a stony track. Many of the tracks are in themselves an eyesore and ski development has caused irreparable, indeed criminal damage. Make sure, as walkers and cyclists, we encourage proper conservation of this wilderness area without the "pressure" of our hobby causing further damage. The Cairngorm region is one of the author's favourite areas in the British Isles, in publishing this book a great deal of trust is placed upon you, the reader, to respect the needs of the region. If all you need is exercise-go elsewhere, but if you appreciate the unique qualities of this region they are yours to enjoy..... carefully!

The maps on the following pages give sufficient detail for exploration of the glens but the Ordnance Survey "Landranger" maps of the region should also be carried if the full geograpical context of the area is to be fully appreciated. These maps are essential if a long tour or cross country expedition is to be undertaken. The more detailed O.S. "Outdoor Leisure" map is excellent for identifying the many forest tracks in the Rothiemurchus and Abernethy forests.

The mountain bike used for the exploration of the glens must be a well maintained machine complete with a few essential spares such as an inner tube and rear wheel axle. A broken bike miles from any-where can be serious. Spare clothing, food etc is best carried in strong panniers on good carriers. Cheap bikes, panniers and carriers simply will not last. Front panniers help distribute weight if there is a load to be carried, and help prevent "wheelies". Mudguards are essential. Rucksacks are tiring and upset balance. A heavy pattern tread to the rear wheel is required. The author does not subscribe to the rucksack/no mudguard/bright colours/tearing-around-the-mountains type of mountainbiking. Nor is this "style" in keeping with what the Cairngorms are about. The area is sacred and needs treating as such. This brings the question of mountainbikers'

clothing into consideration. Traditional road cycling gear is unsuitable. High ankle trainers are best on the feet in summer, and summer weight walking boots are best for winter cycling. The modern zipped fleece jacket with waterproof jacket and overtrousers should be taken with spare tops for easily adjusting body temperature. The wearing

7

of a hard helmet is a personal choice - it depends how you ride, where you ride and the value you place on your own head! In any event a thin balaclava will be required under a helmet in winter - or a thick one in place of a helmet. Also good waterproof gloves are essential. Fingers and ears can get painfully cold on a long descent at -5°C! Protection against exposure should be as for mountain walking. Remember many of the glens are as high as English hilltops. The road cyclists longs - or shorts - will suffice for most conditions but in severe winter cold hiking breeches are perfectly suitable for cycling - and warmer.

The walker has had much previously written about what to wear and carry. Obviously full water-proofs, spare warm clothing, spare food etc should be taken. In winter conditions routes such as the Feshie -Geldie Link can be a major, committing expedition, never to be attempted alone or by the inexperienced. The following is common to both

mountainbikers and walkers:- A map, this book (!), whistle (and knowledge of its proper use), compass and emergency "rations" should always be carried, also in winter a sleeping bag and cooker should be included even if an overnight stop is not planned. Word of your planned route should be left together with your estimated time of arrival. The bothies should be left tidy and with firewood for the next visitor - don't be too proud to remove someone else's litter. Join the Mountain Bothies Association to help support the maintenance of these simple shelters. It should not be necessary to repeat the Country Code and the Mountain Bike Code, the true lover of the wild places needs peace and space - not rules.

8

River crossings are a major consideration when planning routes in Scotland in general and especially in the Cairngorms where snowmelt from the plateau can turn what is a fordable stream in early morning to a raging torrent by mid afternoon. Rivers can be easier to cross with a bike as the bike can be moved, brakes applied, leant on (!) then the feet can be re-positioned and so on. The procedure is to remove boots and socks, replace boots - make sure you can't drop anything and cross (ouch!) Drain boots well, dry your feet and hopefully your still dry socks will do a bit towards warming your feet up again. Remember snowmelt is cold enough to hurt. Choose a wide shallow point to cross if possible and above all don't take risks.

Ascents on a bike should be tackled steadily in a very low gear and sitting down wherever possible. While front panniers prevent "wheelies" sitting down helps the rear wheel grip. Standing on the pedals causes wheel slip, erosion and is tiring. Pushing a laden mountainbike is no fun and is usually the result of tackling the lower half of a climb standing up, in the wrong gear or too fast.

Descents on a bike can be exhilarating but a fast descent is hard on the bike, the rider and the track if wheels are locked - also falling off is much more spectacular and a helmet may be an idea!

Other users of the tracks need treating with respect - it may be the landowner! Mountainbiking has been banned in many areas in the 'States due to inconsiderate riding. Please don't let this happen in Scotland.

9

The Maps 1

The maps are drawn to depict the most important features to the explorer of these glens. North is always at the top of the map and all maps (apart from detail sketches) are to the same scale - 1km (0.6mile) being shown on each map. An attempt has also been made to make the maps pictorially interesting for the "armchair" mountain biker and walker. A brief explanation of the various features is set out below:-

The tracks:- One of the prime objects of this book is to grade the tracks according, basically, to "roughness". This information is essential to the mountainbiker and useful to the walker. With due respect to the Ordnance Survey one "other road, drive or track" can take twice as long to cycle along as another yet both may be depicted in the same way. My attempt at grading is as below:-

metalled road (not too many of these thankfully!)

good track - hardly rutted - nearly as quick as a road on a bike but boring to walk far on.

the usual rutted "Landrover" track - rough but all easily rideable on a mountainbike - not too boring for a walk.

rough very rutted track nearly all rideable - especially downhill! Can be rougher for walkers than some good paths.

really a walkers path but some are included as mountainbike routes when part of a good 'through' route. Over 50% rideable - depending upon the skill of the cyclist.

Relief is depicted in two ways. The heavy black lines are now a commonly used method of depicting main mountain summits, ridges and spurs thus:—

I have also used contour lines at 50m intervals of height up to about 600m to add "shape" to the glens as mapped and also to give the reader an idea of how much climbing is involved in a day out. (Most of the glens climb remarkably little).

Crags in the high mountains are shown thus:—

.... with major areas of scree shown dotted

Rivers - generally "uncrossable"- are shown as *two lines* whilst streams - generally "crossable" - are shown using a *single line*. Note:-great care is needed crossing even the larger streams. Snowmelt can cause them to rise in hours. Falling in can cause embarrassment at best, exposure or drowning at worst; please don't take risks - besides, you'd get this book wet !!

Loch or lochan

Buildings and significant ruins are shown as a ◣ and bridges rather obviously thus:- ⌗. There are so many trees I wish there were an easier way of drawing them - but there isn't! 🌲 🌲🌲
🌲 🌲 🌲 etc. etc.... (I'm fed up with drawing trees!!)

11

Cairngorms - West

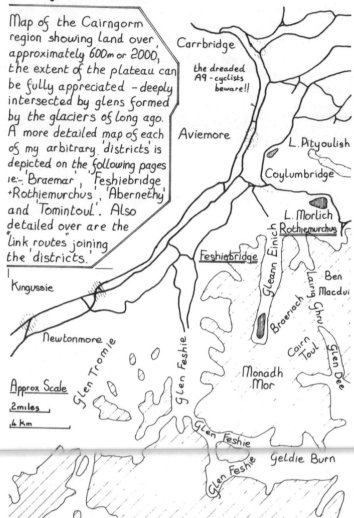

Map of the Cairngorm region showing land over approximately 600m or 2000, the extent of the plateau can be fully appreciated – deeply intersected by glens formed by the glaciers of long ago. A more detailed map of each of my arbitrary 'districts' is depicted on the following pages ie:- 'Braemar', 'Feshiebridge +Rothiemurchus', 'Abernethy' and 'Tomintoul'. Also detailed over are the "Link routes" joining the 'districts.'

Carrbridge

the dreaded A9 - cyclists beware!!

Aviemore

L. Pityoulish

Coylumbridge

L. Morlich

Rothiemurchus

Feshiebridge

Gleann Einich

Ben Macdui

Kingussie

Laing Ghru

Braeriach

Newtonmore

Glen Tromie

Glen Feshie

Cairn Toul

Glen Dee

Approx Scale

Monadh Mor

2miles

4 Km

Glen Feshie

Glen Feshie

Geldie Burn

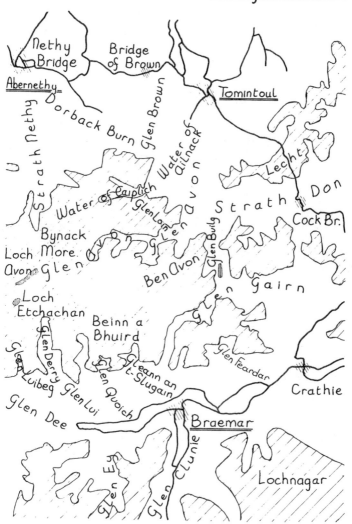

Braemar District

Braemar District

Access:- Access to Braemar from the south or the east is via the A93. The southerly approach from Perth and Blairgowrie passes over the Cairnwell 'ski-road' which can prove "interesting" in winter but is usually cleared for skiers (and the revenue they bring!) The low level approach from Ballater and Balmoral has no such problems. Braemar itself has retained its dignity despite tourism yet still caters for the tourist - perhaps Braemar could teach Aviemore a thing or two! Two scenic approaches to a gem of a village, let's hope it stays just as it is now.

Accommodation:- Braemar boasts two fine hotels, the Fife Arms in the town centre and the Invercauld Arms on the Ballater road. Several small private hotels and guest houses await the visitor. There is a Youth Hostel in Braemar and another at Inverey. A Caravan Club site which also accepts tents lies just "out of town" in Glen Clunie. A Tourist Information Centre is situated in the town centre. Braemar is often 'fully booked' at peak times and watch out for the Braemar Highland Gathering dates.

Geographical Features:- At least ten glens, all draining into the river Dee, radiate from the short section of metalled road from Braemar to Linn of Dee. I have included Glen Ey though strictly out of what I regard as the Cairngorm area because it is a gem. It is with regret I omit Glen Tilt but this beautiful glen really does belong to another area. No such regrets in respect of Glen Callater - a dull north facing glen which belongs to Lochnagar anyway.

Mountains:- The southern heights of the Cairngorm plateau are all accessible from the environs of Braemar However, be warned, the approaches are long - it is here the mountain bike can be used to great advantage but don't forget the distance back to safety at the end of the day.

Rivers :- Few of the rivers are fordable. The infant Dee rises high on the plateau on Braeriach and is soon joined by the Geldie Burn, Lui Water, the Ey Burn, Quoich Water and Clunie Water. Locations of bridges become of vital importance. Rivers also have a tendency to rise in hours due to rain or the melting of unseen snowfields on the high plateau.

Forests:- Some fine remnants of the Caledonian pine forest exist in Glen Derry - in urgent need of protection from browsing deer. Much felling of these magnificent Scots Pine has taken place around Mar Lodge - protection from man needed here! The woods around Invercauld House are beautiful - and teeming with wildlife.

Lochs:- Apart from high mountain lochans and the duckpond above Braemar there aren't any! Don't dare complain — Braemar has just about everything else you could wish for!

Emergency:- Public telephones exist at:-
> Derry Lodge 040934 (these are the O.S.
> Inverey 087892   grid references)
> and Braemar town centre
> A mountain rescue kit is located at Derry Lodge.
> Shelters and bothies, and condition of same is noted on the detail map pages.

Braemar District Routes 1

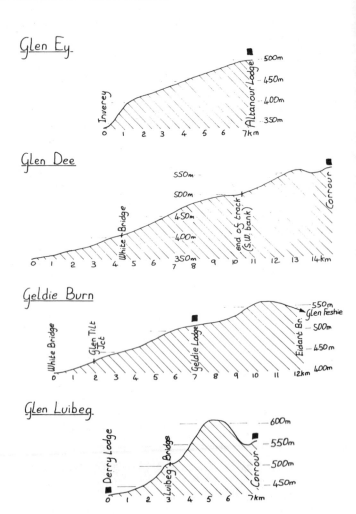

Glen Ey

Inverey — Altanour Lodge

500m, 450m, 400m, 350m

0 1 2 3 4 5 6 7km

Glen Dee

White Bridge — end of track (S.W. bank) — Corrour

550m, 500m, 450m, 400m, 350m

0 1 2 3 4 5 6 7 8 9 10 11 12 13 14km

Geldie Burn

White Bridge — Glen Tilt Jct — Geldie Lodge — Eidart Br. — Glen Feshie

550m, 500m, 450m, 400m

0 1 2 3 4 5 6 7 8 9 10 11 12km

Glen Luibeg

Derry Lodge — Luibeg Bridge — Corrour

600m, 550m, 500m, 450m

0 1 2 3 4 5 6 7km

Glen Lui

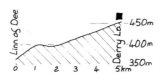

Glen Derry.

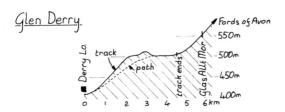

Glen Quoich (West route)

Glen Quoich (East route)

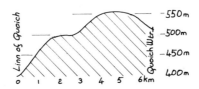

Braemar District Routes 3

Gleann an t-Slugain (valley route)

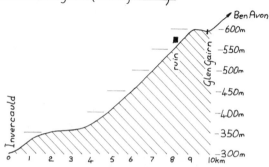

Gleann an t-Slugain (Culardoch route)

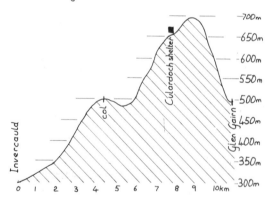

Glen Feardar (ascent via Auchtavan)

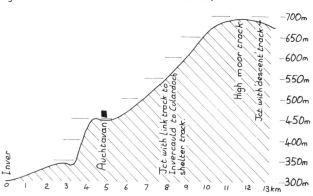

Glen Feardar (descent via Tullochcoy)

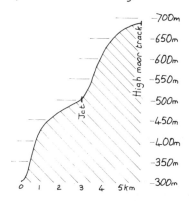

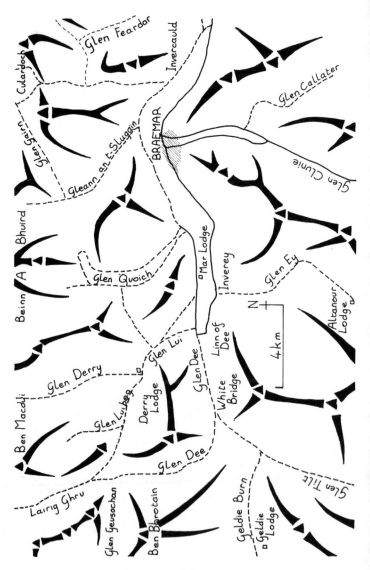

22

Glen Ey lies south of Inverey, a village now, sadly comprising of holiday cottages. Forty families used to inhabit Glen Ey, but now only the ruin of Altanour Lodge watches over the glen. The first part of the track has been 'improved' to an unnecessary standard causing a blot on the landscape. However the curving glen beckons giving superb views of the Cairngorm mountains to the north, Altanour Lodge providing a destination surrounded by the remains of a wood that once provided shelter. The Colonel's Bed, where John Farquharson hid after the Battle of Killiecrankie can be visited on foot if time permits. Altanour Lodge is about 7·5 km (5 miles) from Inverey and twice that distance from Braemar. After a short initial climb the track is almost level, an easy ride with a couple of minor fords. There is no shelter in Glen Ey.

Altanour Lodge

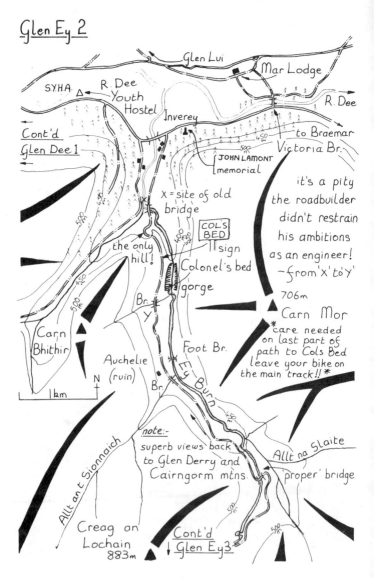

Glen Lui

Mar Lodge

R. Dee

S.Y.H.A. △

R. Dee
Youth
Hostel

Inverey

to Braemar

Cont'd
Glen Dee 1

Victoria Br.

JOHN LAMONT
memorial

X = site of old
bridge

COL'S
BED
sign

it's a pity
the roadbuilder
didn't restrain
his ambitions
as an engineer!
~ from 'X' to 'Y'

the only
hill!

Colonel's bed
gorge

706m

▲

Carn Mor

Br.
Y

* care needed
on last part of
path to Cols Bed
leave your bike on
the main track!! *

Carn
Bhithir

Foot Br.

Auchelie
(ruin)

Ey Burn

N

Br.

1 km

note:-
superb views back
to Glen Derry and
Cairngorm mtns.

Allt na Slaite

'proper' bridge

Allt an t Sionnaich

Creag an
Lochain
883m

Cont'd
↓ Glen Ey 3

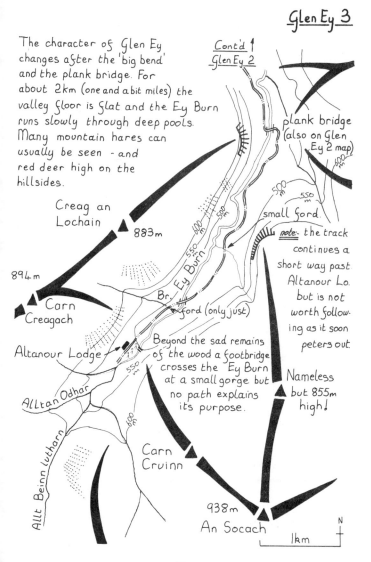

The character of Glen Ey changes after the 'big bend' and the plank bridge. For about 2km (one and a bit miles) the valley floor is flat and the Ey Burn runs slowly through deep pools. Many mountain hares can usually be seen - and red deer high on the hillsides.

Cont'd ↑
Glen Ey 2

plank bridge (also on Glen Ey 2 map)

Creag an Lochain ▲ 883m

small ford.

note:- the track continues a short way past Altanour Lo. but is not worth follow- ing as it soon peters out.

894m

Carn Creagach

Br. Ey Burn

ford (only just)

Altanour Lodge

Beyond the sad remains of the wood a footbridge crosses the Ey Burn at a small gorge but no path explains its purpose.

Nameless but 855m high!

Alltan Odhar

Allt Beinn Iutharn

Carn Cruinn

938m
An Socach

N

1km

25

Glen Dee 1

Glen Dee starts in the Lairig Ghru and continues to Aberdeen! Don't worry—this book only covers the section of interest to the Cairngorm mountain bike enthusiast or walker' ie. from the Lairig Ghru to Inverey. Glen Dee, a worthwhile cycle ride itself, provides the first section of the Braemar to Glen Feshie link route via the wild Geldie Burn, a route not to be undertaken lightly - see next chapter on Geldie Burn - and the Glen Feshie section. The track up the south west bank of the Dee past White bridge runs to a dead end but provides excellent views of the glen and mountains to the north. A boggy walkers path at the opposite side of the valley leads to Corrour bothy via a bridge. There is shelter at Corrour bothy, near Derry Lodge (via Glen Luibeg), or at Ruigh Ealasid 2km south west of White Bridge by the Geldie Burn. There is however no shelter in Glen Dee between Corrour and Inverey.

———————•———————

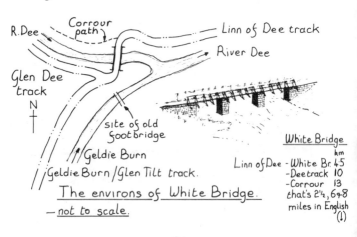

R. Dee

Corrour path

Linn of Dee track

River Dee

Glen Dee track

N

site of old foot bridge

Geldie Burn

Geldie Burn / Glen Tilt track.

The environs of White Bridge.

— not to scale.

White Bridge

km

Linn of Dee - White Br 4.5
        -Dee track 10
        -Corrour 13
that's 2½, 6+8 miles in English (!)

26

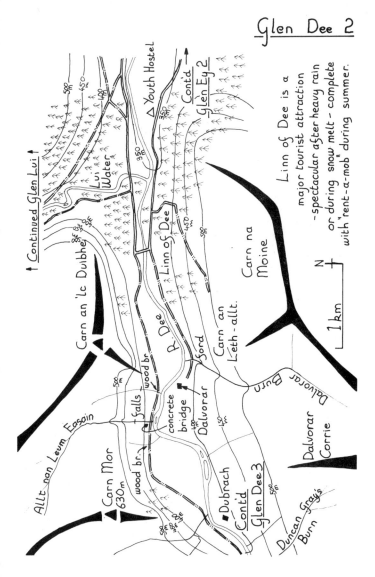

Glen Dee 2

Linn of Dee is a major tourist attraction - spectacular after heavy rain or during snow melt - complete with "rent-a-mob" during summer.

N

1 km

Continued Glen Lui

Carn an 'lc Duibhe

Lui Water

△ Youth Hostel

Glen Ey 2
Cont'd

Linn of Dee

R. Dee

Carn na Moine

Allt nan Leum Easain

Carn Mor
630m

Falls

wood br.

wood br.

concrete bridge

Dalvorar

Sord

Carn an Leth-allt.

Dalvorar Burn

Dubrach

Cont'd
Glen Dee 3

Dalvorar Corrie

Duncan Gray's Burn

27

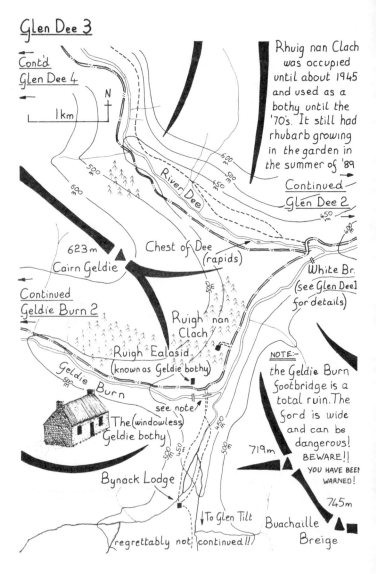

Glen Dee 3

Cont'd
Glen Dee 4
←

N

1 km

Rhuig nan Clach was occupied until about 1945 and used as a bothy until the '70's. It still had rhubarb growing in the garden in the summer of '89

Continued
Glen Dee 2
→

River Dee

600 m
500
450 m
400 m

600
500

623 m
Cairn Geldie

Chest of Dee (rapids)

White Br.
(see Glen Dee 1 for details)

Continued
Geldie Burn 2
←

Ruigh nan Clach

Ruigh Ealasid
(known as Geldie bothy)

Geldie Burn

50 m

see note

450 m

The (windowless)
Geldie bothy

NOTE:-
the Geldie Burn footbridge is a total ruin. The ford is wide and can be dangerous!
BEWARE!!
YOU HAVE BEEN WARNED!

719 m

500
450

500 m

Bynack Lodge

745 m

↓To Glen Tilt

Buachaille
Breige

regrettably not continued!!

28

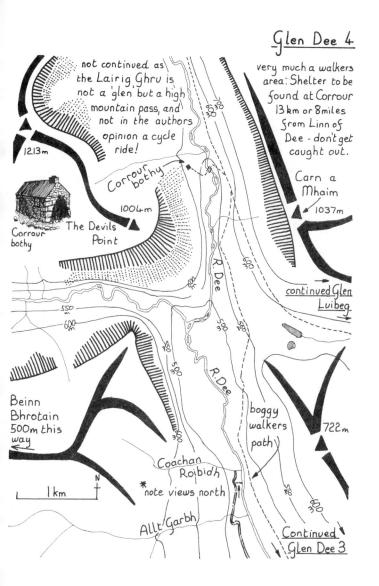

not continued as the Lairig Ghru is not a 'glen' but a high mountain pass, and not in the authors opinion a cycle ride!

1213m

Corrour bothy

The Devils Point   1004m

Corrour bothy

550
600

Beinn Bhrotain 500m this way

1 km

N

very much a walkers area: Shelter to be found at Corrour 13 km or 8 miles from Linn of Dee - don't get caught out.

Carn a Mhaim
1037m

continued Glen Luibeg

722m

R. Dee

boggy walkers path

Coachan Roibidh
* note views north

Allt Garbh

Continued Glen Dee 3

Geldie Burn 1

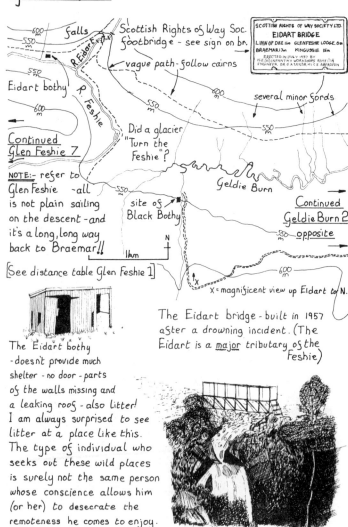

Falls

Scottish Rights of Way Soc.
footbridge - see sign on br.

R. Eidart

vague path - follow cairns

| SCOTTISH RIGHTS OF WAY SOCIETY LTD. |
| EIDART BRIDGE |
| LINN OF DEE 11¾ GLENFESHIE LODGE 6m |
| BRAEMAR 17m   KINGUSSIE 15m |
| ERECTED IN JULY 1957 BY |
| 158 (H) INFANTRY WORKSHOPS REME (TA) |
| ENGINEER, DR G A TAYLOR M.I.C.E ABERDEEN |

Eidart bothy

R. Feshie

several minor fords

Did a glacier "Turn the Feshie"?

Continued Glen Feshie 7

Geldie Burn

NOTE:- refer to Glen Feshie - all is not plain sailing on the descent - and it's a long, long way back to Braemar!!

site of Black Bothy

Continued Geldie Burn 2 opposite

[See distance table Glen Feshie 1]

1km   N

X = magnificent view up Eidart to N.

The Eidart bothy - doesn't provide much shelter - no door - parts of the walls missing and a leaking roof - also litter! I am always surprised to see litter at a place like this. The type of individual who seeks out these wild places is surely not the same person whose conscience allows him (or her) to desecrate the remoteness he comes to enjoy.

The Eidart bridge - built in 1957 after a drowning incident. (The Eidart is a _major_ tributary of the Feshie)

30

NOTE:- To cross from Deeside to Glen Feshie is a committing route over some of the wildest and most desolate moorland in Scotland. The wide, open glen offers no shelter and the rough path passes over the 550m contour, one needs to be physically fit even for a summer crossing. Those who make the crossing are amply rewarded.

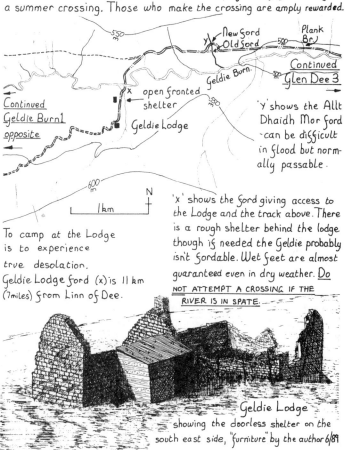

New Ford
Old Ford
Plank Br.

Continued
Glen Dee 3

Geldie Burn.

open fronted shelter

Geldie Lodge

Continued
Geldie Burn1
opposite

'Y' shows the Allt Dhaidh Mor ford - can be difficult in flood but normally passable.

N
1 km

To camp at the Lodge is to experience true desolation.
Geldie Lodge ford (x) is 11 km (7miles) from Linn of Dee.

'x' shows the ford giving access to the Lodge and the track above. There is a rough shelter behind the lodge though if needed the Geldie probably isn't fordable. Wet feet are almost guaranteed even in dry weather. Do NOT ATTEMPT A CROSSING IF THE RIVER IS IN SPATE.

Geldie Lodge
showing the doorless shelter on the south east side, "furniture" by the author 6/89

Glen Luibeg

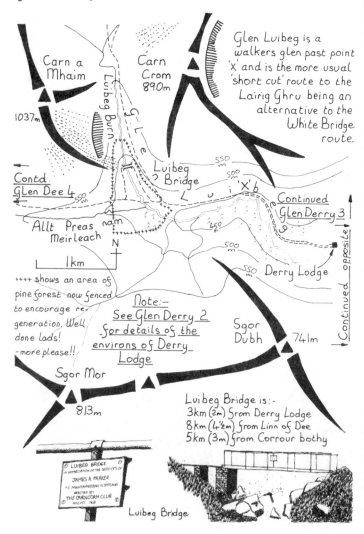

Glen Luibeg is a walkers glen past point 'X' and is the more usual 'short cut' route to the Lairig Ghru being an alternative to the White Bridge route.

Carn a Mhaim

Carn Crom 890m

1037m

Luibeg Burn

Contd. Glen Dee 4

550
500
'X'b

Luibeg Bridge

Continued Glen Derry 3

Allt Preas Meirleach

nam

450m

N

500m
550m

Derry Lodge

1km

++++ shows an area of pine forest now fenced to encourage regeneration. Well done lads! - more please!!

Continued opposite

Note:- See Glen Derry 2 for details of the environs of Derry Lodge

Sgor Dubh

741m

Sgor Mor

813m

Luibeg Bridge is:-
3km (2m) from Derry Lodge
8km (4½m) from Linn of Dee
5km (3m) from Corrour bothy

LUIBEG BRIDGE
IN APPRECIATION OF THE SERVICES OF
JAMES A. PARKER
TO MOUNTAINEERING IN SCOTLAND
ERECTED BY
THE CAIRNGORM CLUB
AUGUST 1948

Luibeg Bridge

32

Glen Lui

Glen Lui is the approach route to the hidden gems of Glen Derry and is all 'cycleable', in fact a bike can be used to great advantage by walkers-reducing the long approach, and the seemingly longer return march. Derry Lodge, or virtually to the end of the flat mid-section of Glen Derry can be comfortably reached by mountain bike, also Glen Luibeg, opposite, can be easily cycled almost to Luibeg Bridge. Derry Lodge is detailed over.

Glen Lui is a wide open glen and deservedly the most popular approach route to the southern Cairngorms.

Continued Glen Derry 3

vague path – aim to the right of the notch on the skyline

opposite

Contd. Glen Quoich 2

shed
dam

Derry Lodge

Continued – opposite

600m

Clais Fhearnaig

Glen

550m

Un-named top 598m high

550m

Lui

ruins

500

Lui Water

500

550 m

A walkers path through Clais Fhearnaig provides an interesting link with Glen Quoich.

500

N

1 km

The best starting point for Glen Lui is here 700m from Linn of Dee

500 450

400

Contd. Glen Dee 2

33

Glen Derry 1

Glen Derry runs north from the confluence of the Luibeg
Burn and the Derry Burn at which point they form the
Lui Water. Situated at the approach to the glen is Derry
Lodge, the much abused and now, sadly boarded-up hunting lodge some 5km (3m) from Linn of Dee. The Scots Pine
forest above Derry Lodge contains some fine trees but is
in desperate need of protection from deer to allow regeneration. Travelling north and once through the woods
the mood of the glen changes to a flat, open
glen where the Derry Dam was once used
to assist timber floating operations.
The upper section of the glen
is a gateway to the heart of
the Cairngorms.

Derry Lodge

The environs of Derry Lodge

beautiful woodland path

Cont'd Glen Derry 3 ↑

Derry Burn

Signpost :- (S.P.)
To Aviemore by the Lairig Ghru
To Nethybridge by Lairig an Laoigh
To Braemar

500   450

500   450

500   450

S.P.

Nature Conservancy shed
superb track — thro' pines

boggy!

Mountain rescue post
Shed - 'phone at 'X'

Derry Lodge

site of bridge

200m approx.

Luibeg Burn

Luibeg Cottage

site of bridge

Continued Glen Luibeg

Continued Glen Lui

Bob Scott's Bothy

450
500

Lui Water

Bob Scotts bothy - built in memory of the game-keeper who lived at Luibeg Cottage. The old bothy near the cottage was burned down.

Bob Scott's

Glen Derry 3

↑ Continued Glen Avon 3 ↑

983m

Glas Allt Mor

Left hand path to Loch Etchachan - right hand path to Fords of Avon via the Lairig an Laoigh - not a cycle ride but an excellent 'through' mountain pass for walkers.

major ford in flood!

Lochan Uaine - one of many!

Craig Derry 865m

Derry Cairngorm

The glen is 'cycleable' up to 'X'

Derry Burn

Beinn Bhreac 931m

X

550

the visitor to Glen Derry is rewarded by fine views north into the mountains

550

Derry Dam

550
500

After a climb through the woods the track drops here to the flat mid-section of the glen

890m

Carn Crom

500m

Meall an Lundain 777m

walkers path through fine Scots pines

550
30
550

500m to Derry Lodge from 'y'

1km

N

Glen Luibeg   y   Glen Lui

36

Glen Quoich provides an interesting excursion for both walker and mountainbiker. Starting with an exploration of the Linn of Quoich with its picturesque waterfall and unsafe bridge (!) some fine remnants of the Caledonian forest can be seen. The glen has both a high level and a low level track with two "interesting" (!) river crossings linking the two. The better track is the low level route up the south west side of Quoich Water, returning by the same route if the fords are impassable, or by the rougher high level route (which does provide good views over the glen) if a successful crossing can be accomplished. A bulldozed road continues almost to the top of Beinn a Bhuird. This is an abomination. An unforgivable scar on the landscape. Landrovers do not belong on the high tops no matter what reason or excuse is given by the builders of these roads. Communication, estate management, revenue from the deer stalkers may be necessary to maintain the estates and, almost by accident, maintain the wild places, but NO-ONE has the god given right to inflict scars on the landscape such as this road. I do not include this route, not only because it is not a "glen", but on principle. Phew! That's got that lot of my chest! I'll calm down now— with a sketch— then a couple of maps of this fine glen.

The unsafe bridge
Linn of Quoich.

Glen Quoich 2

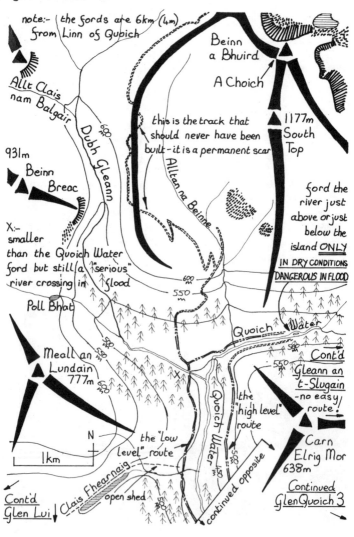

note:- the fords are 6km (4m) from Linn of Quoich

Allt Clais nam Balgair

Beinn a Bhuird

A Choich

Dubh Gleann

600

this is the track that should never have been built - it is a permanent scar

Alltan na Beinne

1177m South Top

931m Beinn Breac

ford the river just above or just below the island **ONLY** IN DRY CONDITIONS **DANGEROUS IN FLOOD**

X:- smaller than the Quoich Water ford but still a "serious" river crossing in flood

Poll Bhat

600
550

Quoich Water

Meall an Lundain 777m

X

the "high level" route

Cont'd Gleann an t-Slugain -no easy route!

Quoich Water

550

N

1km

the "low level" route

550

Carn Elrig Mor 638m

Clais Fhearnaig

open shed

Cont'd Glen Lui

continued opposite

Continued Glen Quoich 3

38

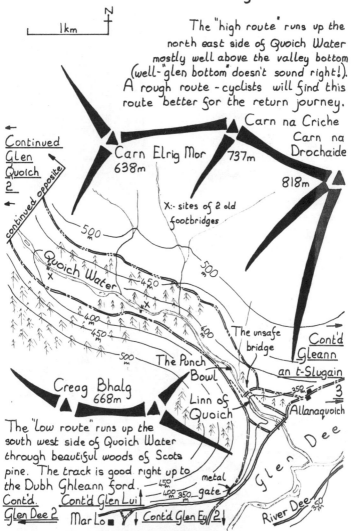

N

1km

The "high route" runs up the
north east side of Quoich Water
mostly well above the valley bottom
(well-"glen bottom" doesn't sound right!).
A rough route - cyclists will find this
route better for the return journey.

Carn na Criche

Carn na
Drochaide

Carn Elrig Mor   737m
638m
                              818m

Continued
Glen
Quoich
2

continued opposite

X:- sites of 2 old
footbridges

500
m

Quoich Water
X
                    500
450
m

400
m
450
m
                              400
500
m   The unsafe   Cont'd
            The Punch   bridge   Gleann
            Bowl   an t-Slugain

Creag Bhalg   350
668m   Linn of   m   3
                Quoich   Allanaquoich

The "low route" runs up the
south west side of Quoich Water
through beautiful woods of Scots
pine. The track is good right up to
the Dubh Ghleann ford.   450
Cont'd.   400 350
Glen Dee 2 Cont'd Glen Lui metal
            Mar Lo ■ gate
                    Cont'd Glen Ey 2

Glen Dee

River Dee   350
m

Gleann an t-Slugain 1

This section not only covers the above named glen (which to be honest is a bit rough for cycling beyond the wood) but the fine link route to the remote Glen Gairn via the high shoulder of Culardoch. Gleann an t-Slugain provides the walker with a long approach march to Ben Avon or, turning right, into the head of Glen Gairn. The area around Invercauld House has many tracks so care is needed in navigation. The woods are teeming with red deer

The Invercauld woods

and red squirrels. Also shown on the maps is the "back road" route to Linn of Quoich but beware of a very large Highland bull which resides near Alltdourie cottage!

Invercauld Bridge

Near Invercauld House

The Culardoch shelter is a door-less stable about 1km below the highest point of the high route to Glen Gairn. Some 10 or 15m north of the shelter an indistinct start to the walkers path to Glen Gairn via Allt na Claise Moire may be found. This is a committing route as the head of Glen Gairn is remote.

Easter snow at the Culardoch shelter (7.5km from Invercauld Br.)

Continued Glen Gairn

The Invercauld - Glen Gairn Link

The climb X-X is the most sustained gradient in this book!

1km ↑N

650 m
600 m
550 m
▲ Clachdhu

River Gairn

550 m
600 m
650 m
700 m

550 m

600 m
600 m
700 m

Culardoch 900m

Fine views of Lochnagar from here.

862 m

600 m
650 m

The Shelter ▸◂ Contd Gleann.... etc (1) 3 ↓

41

Gleann an t-Slugain 3

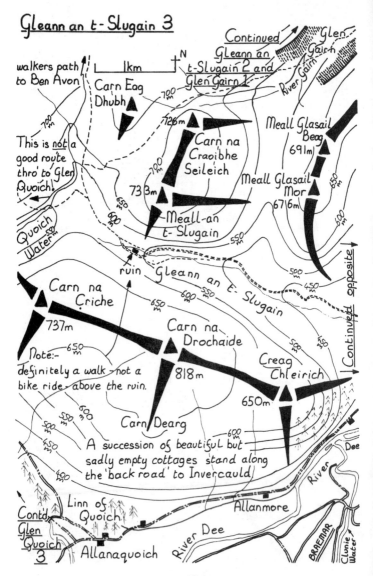

walkers path to Ben Avon

Carn Eag Dhubh

700 m

This is *not* a good route thro' to Glen Quoich!

700 m

Quoich Water

Continued
Gleann an t-Slugain 2 and Glen Gairn 1

Glen Gairn

River Gairn

726 m

Carn na Craoibhe Seileich

Meall Glasail Beag
691m

Meall Glasail Mor
676m

600 m

650 m

600 m

500 m

450 m

Continued opposite

733 m

Meall-an t-Slugain

600 m

650 m

550 m

Gleann an t-Slugain

550 m

ruin

Carn na Criche

737m

650 m

650 m

600 m

550 m

Note:- definitely a walk — not a bike ride — above the ruin.

550 m

600 m

500 m

450 m

Carn na Drochaide

818m

Carn Dearg

500 m

Creag Chleirich

650m

A succession of beautiful but sadly empty cottages stand along the 'back road' to Invercauld

600 m

Dee

Allanmore

River

River Dee

Cont'd Glen Quoich 3

Linn of Quoich

Allanaquoich

BRAEMAR

Clunie Water

1km

N

42

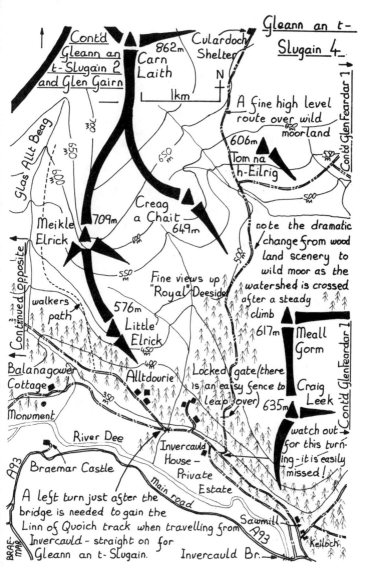

Cont'd
Gleann an
t-Slugain 2
and Glen Gairn

862m
Carn
Laith

Culardoch
Shelter

1km

N

A fine high level
route over wild
moorland

606m
Tom na
h-Eilrig

Contd GlenFeardar 1

Glas Allt Beag

650
600

709m
Meikle
Elrick

Creag
a Chait
649m

note the dramatic
change from wood
land scenery to
wild moor as the
watershed is crossed
after a steady
climb

Continued opposite

walkers
path

576m
Little
Elrick

Fine views up
"Royal" Deeside

617m
Meall
Gorm

Contd GlenFeardar 1

Balnagower
Cottage

Monument

Alltdourie

Locked gate (there
is an easy fence to
leap over)

Craig
Leek
635m

watch out
for this turn-
ing - it is easily
missed!

River Dee

Braemar Castle

A93

main road

Invercauld
House -
Private
Estate

Sawmill
A93

Keiloch

A left turn just after the
bridge is needed to gain the
Linn of Quoich track when travelling from
Invercauld - straight on for
Gleann an t-Slugain.

BRAE-
MAR

Invercauld Br.

Glen Feardar 1

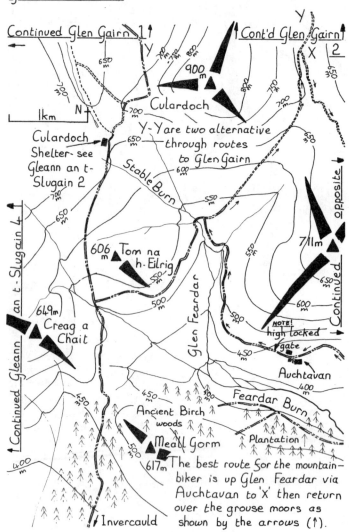

Continued Glen Gairn 1 ↑

Cont'd Glen Gairn 2 ↑

900m

Culardoch

Y–Y are two alternative through routes to Glen Gairn

Culardoch Shelter- see Gleann an t-Slugain 2

Continued opposite →

Stable Burn

711m

650m

606m Tom na h-Eilrig

Continued →

NOTE! high locked gate

Continued Gleann an t-Slugain 4 ↑

649m Creag a Chait

Glen Feardar

Auchtavan

Feardar Burn

Ancient Birch woods

Plantation

Meall Gorm 617m

The best route for the mountain-biker is up Glen Feardar via Auchtavan to 'X' then return over the grouse moors as shown by the arrows (↑).

↓ Invercauld

1km N↑

44

Glen Feardar is a glen that died. Most of the farms are alas empty, even the church - still with its now silent bell - is now a barn However this little explored glen has fine ancient birchwoods in its lower reaches, giving way to high grouse moors where only grouse, mountain hare and deer are seen. Few people frequent this area. The route passes first through the farms and birchwoods and climbs considerably to the higher reaches of the Feardar Burn. The high moor track can be gained to continue to Glen Gairn, link up with the Glen Gairn/Invercauld track or return to Inver via the high moor track of Bad nan Cuileag.

Auchtavan

high exposed moor track

Bad nan Cuileag

Carn Moine an Tighearn 643m

600m
650m

Two high gates (not locked)

Leac Ghorm 593m

Continued opposite ↑

Craig Nordie 488m Follow the arrows (↑) for a 16 km (10m) circuit.

Feardar Burn

Balmore

Tullochcoy A93

Crathie 4km

Church Inver

Felagie Burn

River Dee

Inver Hotel 600m

45

Feshiebridge and Rothiemurchus District

Feshiebridge and Rothiemurchus District

Access:- Dead easy! The B970 runs parallel with the A9 from Feshiebridge to Coylumbridge and the "ski road" to Loch Morlich from Coylumbridge completes the metalled roads bordering this area. Part of the route up Glen Feshie is also metalled. The less said about Aviemore the better but suffice to say it provides an extremely useful feature - a railway station. Catch the train to Aviemore complete with mountainbike and tent, and you are a free man (or woman!).

Accommodation:- Aviemore has everything, and is in my opinion a disastrous mess — apart from the above station and the obligatory tourist information office, there is also a Youth Hostel - and another at Loch Morlich. There is a private hostel in Glen Feshie. An excellent Forestry Commission camp/caravan site is situated at Loch Morlich though it does become a bit too busy at peak times. There is another camp site, and a hotel, at Coylumbridge.

Geographical Features:- The area is bounded and dominated by Glen Feshie, split in two by the dark defile of Gleann Einich, and also bounded by the beautiful Rothiemurchus Forest, — Loch Morlich, and the road down to Coylumbridge to form my arbitrary 'District'. West of Glen Feshie merits further exploration but has to be beyond the bounds of this book. All the rivers in this region drain into the mighty River Spey. ("Strathspey" please - not the Anglicized "Spey Valley"!)

Mountains:- Gleann Einich and some of the Rothiemurchus tracks can be used by mountainbikers to advantage to gain access to the northern summits and corries. The approaches are not as long as those on the Braemar side. The Cairngorm mountains cannot be fully appreciated from the A9 and Coylumbridge unless they have first been explored at close quarters, that is on foot!

Rivers:— This District is dominated by the Spey and its tributaries, the largest of which is the Feshie. The lower reaches of the Feshie are well provided with bridges but problems lie in the upper glen - a choice between two major (usually impossible) fords and a narrow path above the river necessitating carrying a bike on ones shoulder (there isn't room to wheel it!) More details of these delights on Glen Feshie 4. The Cairngorm Club Footbridge over the Einich and the Luineag bridge near the outflow of Loch Morlich solve any problems elsewhere. Other fords are of a minor nature except in very severe flood conditions.

Forests:— The Rothiemurchus Forest is the finest remaining area of the once great Caledonian Forest. Efforts are being made to preserve this great natural asset and its protection is of paramount importance. The deer-grazed pines of Glen Feshie don't stand a chance with the present number of deer. Some pathetic attempts at protecting young pines in Glen Feshie with 1m (3') high fences have produced hedge sized examples. The mixed woodlands around Loch Eilein can be readily explored by bike or on foot.

Lochs:— Loch Morlich is the largest and even sports a beach. It has become a water sports centre in recent years and is bordered by roadside picnic tables car parks and sign posts. By contrast Loch Einich - ink black under the surrounding crags is the epitome of all that is wild and remote - its setting being second only to Loch Avon. Loch Eilein is a gem - a beautiful loch - complete with castle set amongst woodland, it has to be seen to be believed!

Emergency:— Public telephones exist at :—

Loch Morlich 976097 (these are O.S.
Coylumbridge 915108   grid references)
Feshiebridge 853044

Shelters, bothies and condition of same — see detail maps.

Feshiebridge and Rothiemurchus District Routes 1

Glen Feshie

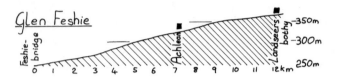

Drakes Bothy

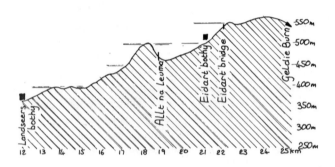

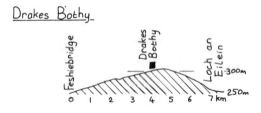

Feshiebridge and Rothiemurchus District Routes 2

Loch an Eilein

The route around Loch an Eilein is nearly flat so a gradient profile would appear as a straight Line! O.K. if you insist :- "——————————"

Gleann Einich

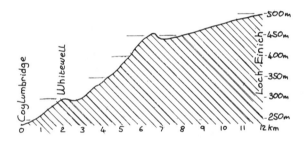

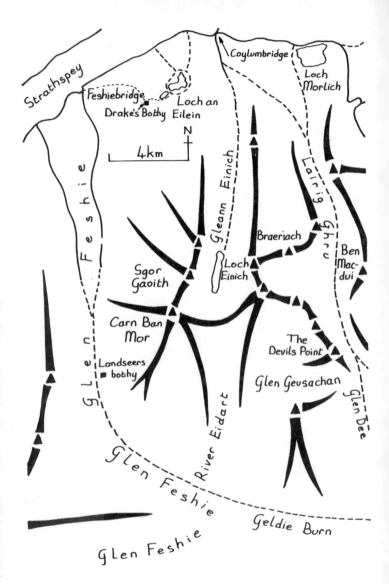

Strathspey

Coylumbridge

Loch Morlich

Feshiebridge
Drake's Bothy
Loch an Eilein

N
4km

Gleann Einich

Lairig Ghru

Braeriach

Ben Mac-dui

Sgor Gaoith

Loch Einich

Carn Ban Mor

Landseers bothy

The Devils Point

Glen Geusachan

Glen Dee

River Eidart

Glen Feshie

Geldie Burn

Glen Feshie

Glen Feshie

The wide open spaces that are Glen Feshie sweep south from Feshiebridge to the great fork in the glen just south of the Landseer bothy Thereafter the main glen narrows between steep scree slopes and many tumbling waterfalls. The floor of the glen rises and the Allt na Leuma is crossed at a dramatic gorge. A mile or so further on the Eidart bridge is crossed and the vast wilderness of the "Feshie-Geldie Link opens up. The Feshie swings south and west into its own private wilderness, the vast no-mans-land between the Cairngorm mountains and Blair Atholl - truly undramatic unadulterated wilderness. Glen Feshie is long - very long, and to assist a table of distances follows.

From: ⟶	Feshiebridge		or Achlean		Notes:-
To: ↓					① remember-the
	km	m	km	m	Feshie-Geldie
Achlean	7	4			Link is a serious
Landseers bothy	12	7	5	3	bike ride or walk
Allt na Leuma	19	12	12	7	-do your homework
Eidart bothy	21	13	14	9	before setting off
Eidart Bridge	22	14	15	9	② There was a
Geldie Lodge	27	17	20	12	move to build a
Geldie bothy	32	20	25	15	Feshie-Geldie road.
White Bridge	34	21	27	17	HANDS OFF!! this
Linn of Dee	39	24	32	20	rare wilderness!!
Braemar	49	30	42	25	

There is shelter at Landseers bothy (plus a fire); Eidart bothy (not much good!); Geldie Lodge (across the Geldie and doorless!) Geldie bothy (no door or windows). Refer Geldie Burn 1 for more details.

Glen Feshie 2

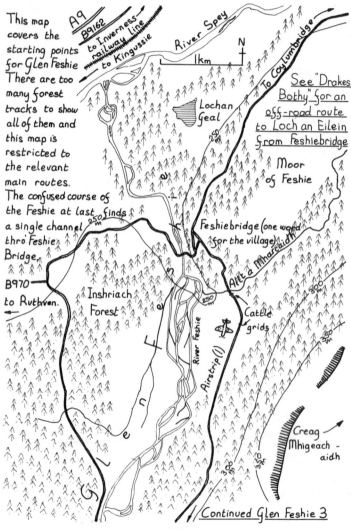

This map covers the starting points for Glen Feshie. There are too many forest tracks to show all of them and this map is restricted to the relevant main routes. The confused course of the Feshie at last finds a single channel thro Feshie Bridge.

A9
B9162
to Inverness railway line
to Kingussie

River Spey

N
1km

Lochan Geal

To Coylumbridge

See "Drakes Bothy" for an off-road route to Loch an Eilein from Feshiebridge

Moor of Feshie

250 m

Feshiebridge (one word for the village)

Allt a Mharcaidh

B970 to Ruthven.

Inshriach Forest

Glen Feshie

River Feshie

250

Cattle grids

300

Airstrip(1)

320

Creag Mhigeach-aidh

300

300

Continued Glen Feshie 3

Glen Feshie 3

Many forest tracks omitted to the west of Glen Feshie - they don't form good thro' glen routes.

Contd.

Glen Feshie 2

Balachroick

The wide open spaces of Glen Feshie are a mountainbiker's paradise.

River Feshie

Balna scriten

300

Tolvah

300

Coran-stilbeg

Corarnstilmore

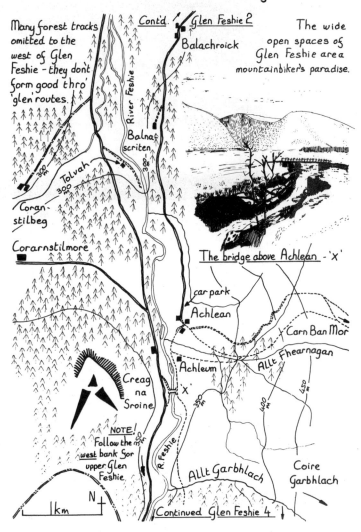

The bridge above Achlean - 'X'

car park

Achlean

Carn Ban Mor

Allt Fhearnagan

400 m

450 m

Achleum

Creag na Sroine

X

R. Feshie

350 m

400 m

NOTE! Follow the west bank for upper Glen Feshie

Allt Garbhlach

Coire Garbhlach

1 km

N

Continued Glen Feshie 4

55

Cont'd Glen Feshie 3

Coire
Garbhlach

Meall nan
Sleac

track
to the high
plateau.

Carnachuin
Mon

X

Coire Cool

Glenfeshie
Lodge

R. Feshie

Landseers Bothy
Landseers chimney

The best route up
the glen follows the
west bank up to 'X' then
crosses to the bothy

918m
Druim
nam Bo

N

1km

track washed away
- only a narrow
path above the
river remains!

Lochan
nam Bo

Slochd

Allt Lorgaidh

precarious section
of narrow path over
scree, rock and
stream - not
for the
faint
hearted.

the Slochd
track and
Allt Lorg-
aidh path
lead to
the source
of the Feshie

these are
three major
fords. Exceptional
drought essential for
any attempt at a
crossing - don't
risk it !!

Continued

Glen Feshie 6

This is the exciting section of Glen Feshie for both mountainbikers and walkers alike. The Feshie winds among glacial deposits on an ever changing course, which has washed away the original track up the steep east bank and a new track crossing the Feshie no less than three times rejoins the old track higher up the glen. The path clings to the hillside being no more than a ledge on a steep slope of scree in places. No problem for walkers (unless snow lies deep) but the intrepid cyclist has to be able to carry his bike for a couple of 100metre

Ruigh Aiteachain

stretches. I have managed this with a mountainbike full of camping gear having made the crossing from the Geldie. If you have any doubts approach from the Glen Feshie side rather than from the Geldie as it isn't as far to turn back.

The Landseer Bothy, correctly Ruigh Aiteachain, is situated near the artist Landseer's cottage, the chimney of which still remains. The bothy is maintained by the Mountain Bothies Association and provides basic shelter with a sleeping platform in the roof. The steep track via the magnificent Coire Garbhlach goes up onto the high plateau but Landrovers do not belong up there. The high plateau is a sacred wilderness. The track via Slochd and the walkers path via Allt Lorgaidh go almost to the source of the Feshie but are beyond the scope of this book.

Ancient pines near the great fork in the glen where Allt Lorgaidh joins the Feshie.

Glen Feshie 6

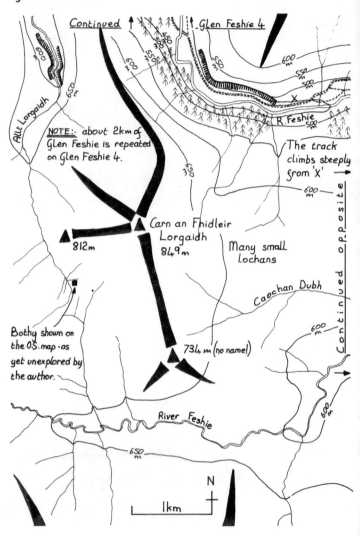

Continued ↑↑ Glen Feshie 4

600 m

650 m

Allt Lorgaidh

600 m

450 550 350 400 500

550 500 600 m

550 500 X

R. Feshie 500

NOTE:- about 2km of Glen Feshie is repeated on Glen Feshie 4.

350

The track climbs steeply from 'X' →

600 m

▲ 812m

▲ Carn an Fhidleir Lorgaidh 849m

Many small lochans

Caochan Dubh

600 m

Bothy shown on the O.S. map · as yet unexplored by the author.

▲ 734m (no name!)

600 m

Continued opposite →

River Feshie

650 m

N

1km

58

Allt Coire Bhlair

See detail below

See Geldie Burn 1 for details of the Eidart bothy and the continuation to Braemar, also Eidart Br.

ford

600 m

550 m

500 m

R. Feshie

500 m

Eidart bothy

550 m

River Eidart

vague cairned path

600 m

to the Geldie

550 m

The wild but surprisingly green expanse around the shallow glen of the Geldie is encountered beyond the Eidart

opposite

600 m

River Feshie

Continued Geldie Burn 1

source of the Geldie

Continued

600 m

path to nowhere

600 m

550 m

site of Black Bothy

Allt Coire Bhlair

X = best view of falls

complete with falls

600 m

Here the Feshie flows fast in a steep ravine.

Allt na Sumaig

Allt nan Soithichean

550 m

500 m

higher track for cyclists

walkers path

450 m

450 m

600 m

550 m

ford via island – danger in flood!!

500 m

path to the Geldie

X R. Feshie

Detail of the Allt Coire Bhlair crossing

Drake's Bothy 1

The Drake's Bothy route is included as an important off-road link in the "Cairngorm Circuit" (details later!) as it cuts out a stretch of metalled road between Feshiebridge and Coylumbridge. It also provides a series of pleasant forest tracks, the bothy itself, and a good 'cycleable' footpath linking up with Loch an Eilein (refer L: an E. 1 and 2), thence via the Cairngorm Club Footbridge (Glen Einich 1) or the Slugan, or Glen More to Ryvoan. Alternatively the bothy forms an ideal extension to the rather short circuit of Loch-an-Eilein.
The bothy is the property of the Nature Conservancy Council and its correct name is "Inshriach Bothy" according to a sign under the eaves of the corrugated roof.

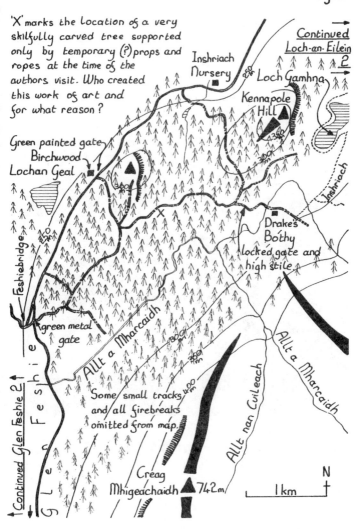

'X' marks the location of a very skilfully carved tree supported only by temporary (?) props and ropes at the time of the authors visit. Who created this work of art and for what reason?

Continued Loch-an-Eilein 2

Inshriach Nursery

Loch Gamhna

Kennapole Hill

Green painted gate Birchwood Lochan Geal

Inshriach

Drake's Bothy locked gate and high stile

Feshiebridge

green metal gate

Allt a Mharcaidh

Allt a Mharcaidh

Allt nan Cuileach

Some small tracks and all firebreaks omitted from map.

Continued Glen Feshie 2

Glen Feshie

Creag Mhigeachaidh

742m

N

1 km

61

Loch an Eilein 1

O.K. so it's not a glen! Loch an Eilein is such a beautiful place it deserves a mention – two whole pages in fact! It comes complete with tourist information centre, car park and often quite a few people. However, pick a quiet time to walk around its shore or combine it with a cycle ride from Coylumbridge via Blackpark and back via Lochan Deo and the Cairngorm Club footbridge. It is an ideal introduction to mountainbiking and links up with the even easier Rothiemurchus Lodge track. (See Gleann Einich 2)

Loch an Eilein

Personal note:- My first ever mountainbike ride was from Coylumbridge to the Cairngorm Club footbridge and Loch an Eilein. This area has therefore special memories, and marked the start of a new activity for me (in addition to road cycling and mountain walking). From that first trip a wider interest in the Cairngorm region as a whole (not just its mountains) developed - hence this book.

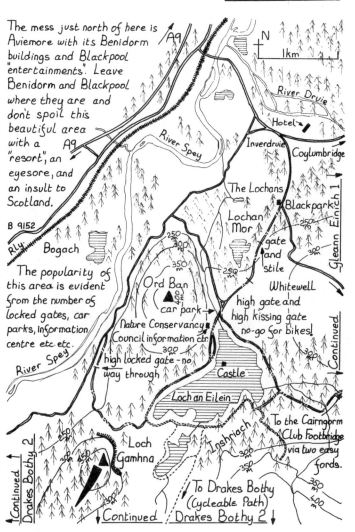

The mess just north of here is Aviemore with its Benidorm buildings and Blackpool "entertainments". Leave Benidorm and Blackpool where they are and don't spoil this beautiful area with a "resort", an eyesore, and an insult to Scotland.

The popularity of this area is evident from the number of locked gates, car parks, information centre etc. etc.

A9

N

1km

River Druie

Hotel

River Spey

Inverdruie

Coylumbridge

A9

The Lochans

Blackpark

Lochan Mor

Gleann Einich 1

B 9152

Rly.

Bogach

250

300

350 m

250

gate and stile

Whitewell

Ord Ban 400 m

car park

Nature Conservancy Council information ctr.

high gate and high kissing gate no-go for bikes!

River Spey

300

high locked gate - no way through

Castle

300

Continued

Loch an Eilein

Loch Gamhna

250 350 m

250

300 m

Inshriach

300

250

To the Cairngorm Club Footbridge via two easy fords.

350 400 m

To Drakes Bothy (cycleable Path)

Continued Drakes Bothy 2

Continued Drakes Bothy 2

Gleann Einich 1

The trek or ride to Gleann Einich has four alternative starting points :- 1/ From the car park at Loch an Eilein via this beautiful lochan; 2/ From Whitewell, the shortest route; 3/ From Coylumbridge, following the river all the way from the road, and 4/ From the outflow of Loch Morlich over the Cairngorm Club footbridge. From the pleasant woodland scenery to the grandeur of Loch Einich all in a day. Whitewell is 10km from Loch Einich— thats 6 miles and there is no shelter in Gleann Einich, so if it rains......tough!!

Cont'd Milton Burn↑

An Beanaidh

River Luineag

250 m

Cont'd Loch an Eilein 2↑

300

cattle grid

locked gate and stile

The Cairngorm Club footbridge

Whitewell

Loch an E.

300

Cairngorm Club F.Br.

high gate -very high stile!

350

high locked gate

kissing gate too small for bikes - no stile.

Lochan Deo

350 m

250

100

here the old track has been washed away cyclists take the high track. Cont'd Gleann Einich 2↓

Rothiemurchus Lodge

64

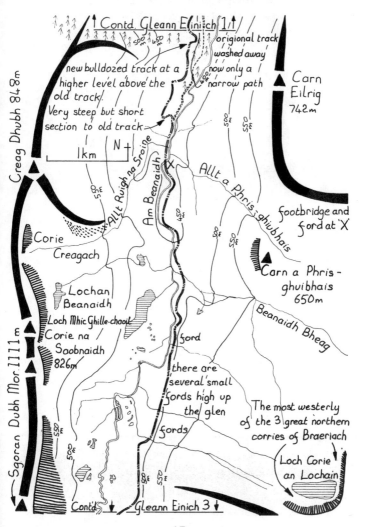

Contd. Gleann Einich 1

original track washed away now only a narrow path

new bulldozed track at a higher level 'above' the old track.
Very steep but short section to old track

1 km   N

Carn Eilrig 742m

Creag Dhubh 848m

Allt Ruigh na Sroine

Am Beanaidh

Allt a Phris-ghuibhais

X

footbridge and ford at 'X'

Corie Creagach

Lochan Beanaidh

Loch Mhic Ghille-chaoil

Corie na Saobnaidh 826m

Sgoran Dubh Mor 1111m

Carn a Phris-ghuibhais 650m

Beanaidh Bheag

ford

there are several 'small' fords high up the glen

fords

The most westerly of the 3 great northern corries of Braeriach

Loch Corie an Lochain

Contd↓ Gleann Einich 3 ↓

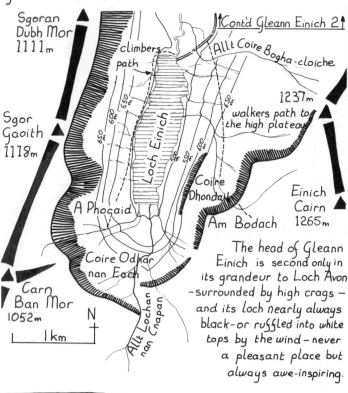

Gleann Einich 3

Sgoran
Dubh Mor
1111m

↑Cont'd Gleann Einich 2↑

climbers
path

Allt Coire Bogha-cloiche

1237m

walkers path to
the high plateau

Sgor
Gaoith
1118m

Loch Einich

650m
600m
550m

550m
600m
650m

A Phocaid

Coire
Dhondail

Einich
Cairn
1265m

Am Bodach

Carn
Ban Mor
1052m

Coire Odhar
nan Each

N

1 km

Allt Lochan nan Cnapan

The head of Gleann
Einich is second only in
its grandeur to Loch Avon
-surrounded by high crags -
and its loch nearly always
black-or ruffled into white
tops by the wind - never
a pleasant place but
always awe-inspiring.

The Footbridge

Even snow in the gullies fails to lighten the gloom on a stormy
winters day at Loch Einich.

———————— " ————————

A few days spent in the company of the mountains and the
vast landscapes of the Cairngorms can place our every-
day problems and pressures in true perspective. We
can return to our work not only refreshed but with
an almost smug inner satisfaction only the lover of the
mountains and these wild places can understand. When
others are rushing around we can let our minds flash back
to the wild places and to time spent there, and instead
of letting life's pressures overcome us, we can stand
back from them, detached, knowing secretly how small
these problems really are in the true vast scale of
life and landscape. Loch Einich is one such place.

Abernethy District

Abernethy District

Access:- Turn off the A9 just north of Aviemore then take the A95 soon turning off through Boat of Garten thence via the B970 to Nethy Bridge, or- follow the B970 all the way from Coylumbridge via the beautiful Pityoulish to Nethy Bridge. Trains run to Aviemore from which one can cycle via the Slugan Pass, The Green Lochan or Loch Garten to Nethy Bridge.

Accommodation:- See Feshiebridge notes for detail (and opinion!) on Aviemore. Better is the Youth Hostel or excellent camp site at Loch Morlich. Nethy Bridge has an hotel, guesthouses, a private hostel and many houses to let

Geographical Features:- The area is based on Strath Nethy with the Dorback Burn its main tributary. The dominant feature is the fine Abernethy Forest - with its ample supply of tracks for mountainbiking or wandering over this undulating area of glacial moraine.

Mountains:- The outlying Meall a Bhuachaille (Shepherds Hill) is almost encircled by the tracks in this section, but the real interest lies higher up Strath Nethy and its link over the Saddle to Glen Avon. Most of the remaining hills in the region are rounded grouse moors.

Rivers:- The River Nethy is the main waterway, collecting the Dorback Burn on its way to the Spey. The Green Lochan however drains into Loch Morlich.

Forests:- The Abernethy Forest represents another fine slice of the ancient Caledonian Forest now preserved by the R.S.P.B. as their Loch Garten reserve. Let us hope this will continue to be protected for all time.

Lochs:- The well known Loch Garten is the main attraction but I prefer the tranquillity of nearby Loch Mallachie or the Green Lochan. The many small lochans are worth a visit.

Emergency:- There are public telephones at Nethybridge and L Morlich (o.s. ref:- 001206 and 974098 respectively). Only Strath Nethy is remote enough to note the relevant shelters.

Milton Burn and Glen More

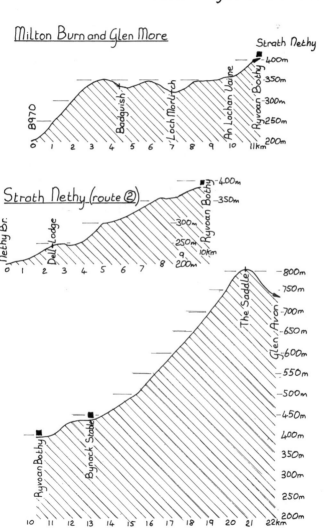

Strath Nethy (route ②)

71

Abernethy District Routes 2

Dorback Burn

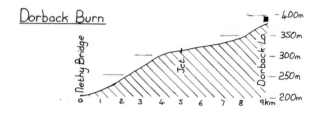

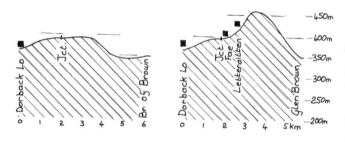

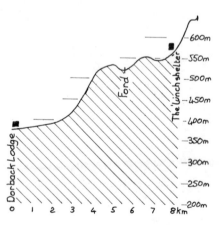

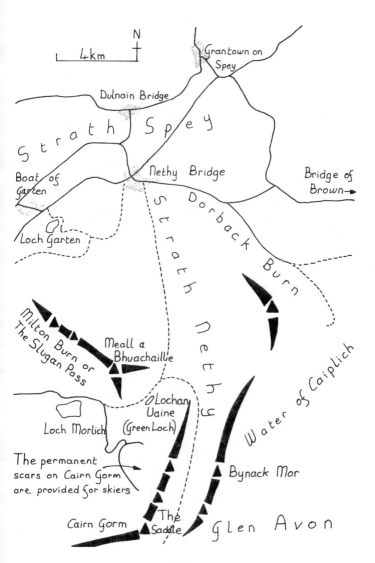

N

4km

Grantown on Spey

Dulnain Bridge

S t r a t h   S p e y

Boat of Garten

Nethy Bridge

Bridge of Brown→

Loch Garten

S t r a t h   D o r b a c k   B u r n

S t r a t h   N e t h y

Milton Burn or The Slugan Pass

Meall a Bhuachaille

W a t e r   o f   C a i p l i c h

Lochan Uaine (Green Loch)

Loch Morlich

The permanent scars on Cairn Gorm are provided for skiers

Bynack Mor

Cairn Gorm

The Saddle

G l e n   A v o n

Milton Burn (The Slugan Pass)

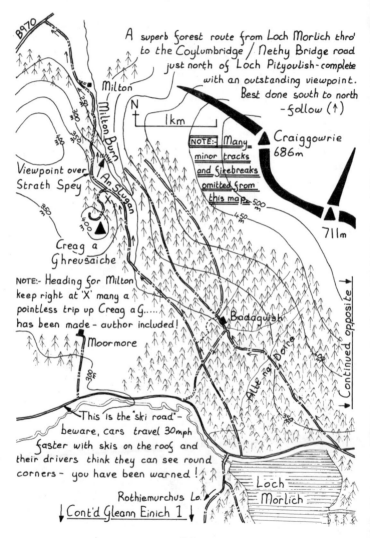

A superb forest route from Loch Morlich thro' to the Coylumbridge / Nethy Bridge road just north of Loch Pityoulish - complete with an outstanding viewpoint. Best done south to north - follow (↑)

B970

Milton

Milton Burn

Viewpoint over Strath Spey

An Slugan

X

NOTE:- Many minor tracks and firebreaks omitted from this map

N
1km

Craiggowrie 686m

711m

Creag a Ghreusaiche

NOTE:- Heading for Milton keep right at 'X' many a pointless trip up Creag a G..... has been made - author included!

Moormore

Badaguish

Allt na Doire

Continued opposite

This is the "ski road" - beware, cars travel 30mph faster with skis on the roof and their drivers think they can see round corners - you have been warned!

Rothiemurchus Lo.

Loch Morlich

↓ Cont'd Gleann Einich 1 ↓

Glen More

Lochan Uaine (the Green Loch) is a local beauty spot attracting a number of walkers out for a short stroll. It is an important link route between Loch Morlich (the 'ski-road', camp site and Youth Hostel) and Strath Nethy, either to walk to the head of Strath Nethy or to explore the Abernethy Forest. A good 'round trip' mountainbiking route from Loch Morlich is to go over the Slugan Pass, north to Nethy Bridge and return via the Abernethy Forest and the Green Loch. See Strath Nethy 3 & 6 for details of the Ryvoan Bothy.

Creagan Gorm
732m

1km   N

very steep!

Continued Strath Nethy 3

Lochan a Chait

Meall a Bhuachaille (Shepherds Hill) 810m

Ryvoan Bothy

Loch a Garbh-choire

Ryvoan Pass

Lochan Uaine

Continued Strath Nethy 3

500 450 400

350

'Phone

Youth Hostel

Continued opposite

Glen More

Loch M.

Forestry Commission Campsite

Glenmore Lodge (National Outdoor Training Centre and Mountain Rescue Post)

The woods of the Abernethy Forest are happily owned and preserved by the Royal Society for the Protection of Birds, the area includes Loch Garten. The Loch Garten area is provided with some superb metalled roads, worth exploration but not within the scope of this book. The Abernethy Forest however _is_ included around the River Nethy and an excellent network of good tracks provide the walker and mountainbiker with a reason to spend 2 or 3 days exploring the area. Red squirrel and roe deer can be observed, especially in the south eastern reaches of the Forest as this area is quieter, away from the link route via the Ryvoan Bothy to Loch Morlich.

Beyond the Bynack Stable the ways divide, one path leading over the Fords of Avon/Lairig an Laoigh route to Glen Derry (a committing high level pass), the other path leading up Strath Nethy to Loch Avon via The Saddle. Only the Strath Nethy route is included and from the Bynack Stable south this is definitely a walk rather than a bike ride. Upper Strath Nethy is slow going and if much exploration is intended beyond the Saddle a start is better made from Glen More in order to reduce the total distance.

Please note this area is extra sensitive to disturbance and within the forest it is vital to keep strictly to the tracks, not drop litter etc.etc. - things I know you wouldn't dream of doing anyway!

The shelter just north of Forest Lodge - see map opposite - bales of straw to sit on and a bike shed behind!! Remember it is private so don't leave _any_ trace of your visit.

..... This shelter has kept me dry more than once!

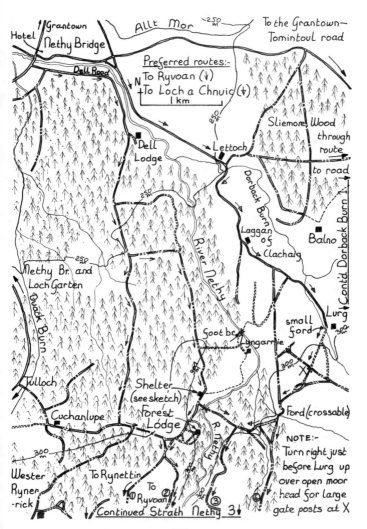

Hotel / Grantown
Nethy Bridge
Allt Mor
To the Grantown–Tomintoul road
Dell Road
Preferred routes:-
To Ryvoan (↓)
To Loch a Chnuic (↓)
1 km
N
250 m
Dell Lodge
Lettoch
Sliemore Wood through route to road
250 m
Dorback Burn
Laggan
Clacharg
Balno
River Nethy
Nethy Br and Loch Garten
250
Quack Burn
Lurg
small ford
Scoot br.
Lyngarrie
300 m
X
Tulloch
Shelter (see sketch)
Forest Lodge
Ford (crossable)
Cuchanlupe
R. Nethy
Contd Dorback Burn
300 m
Wester Ryner-rick
To Rynettin
To Ryvoan
① ② ③ ④
Continued Strath Nethy 3↓

NOTE:-
Turn right just before Lurg up over open moor head for large gate posts at X

77

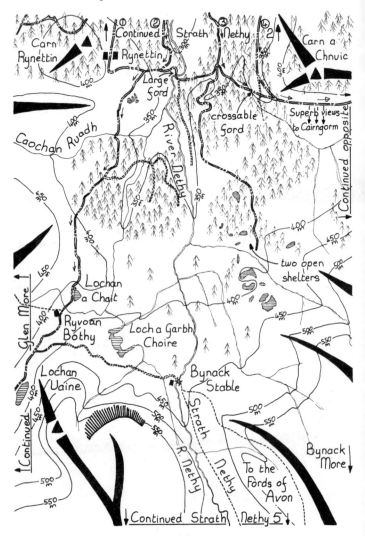

Carn Rynettin

① Continued ② Strath ③ Nethy ④ ②

Rynettin

Carn a Chnuic

Large Ford

400

crossable ford

400

Superb views to Cairngorm

Caochan Ruadh

River Nethy

350

350m

350m

Continued opposite

400

450

500m

two open shelters

450m

350m

450m

Lochan a Chait

Glen More

400

500m

Ryvoan Bothy

Loch a Garbh Choire

400m

550m

Lochan Uaine

Bynack Stable

450m

Continued

400

Strath Nethy

500m

550

R. Nethy

Bynack More

500m

550m

To the Fords of Avon

↓ Continued Strath Nethy 5 ↓

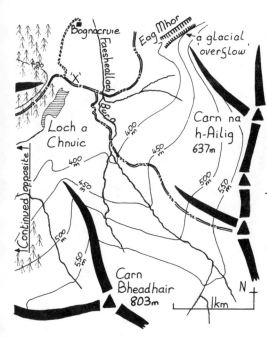

The track up to
Loch a Chnuic
is included
because of
the magnificent
view towards
Cairngorm. This
is, in the authors
opinion, the best
distant view of
Cairngorm of all.
The tracks beyond
the loch are an
eyesore but the
trip to point 'X'
is well worth
the effort.

Reflection at Loch a Chnuic.

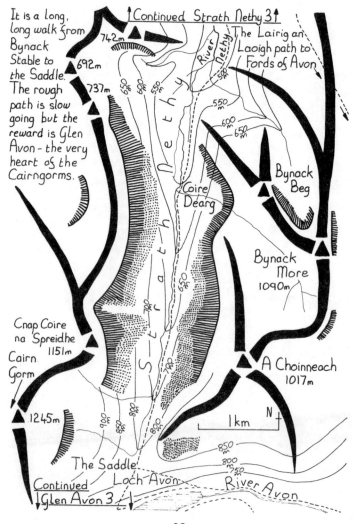

It is a long, long walk from Bynack Stable to the Saddle. The rough path is slow going but the reward is Glen Avon – the very heart of the Cairngorms.

↑Continued Strath Nethy 3↑

742m

692m

737m

650
600
550
550

600
650

The Lairig an Laoigh path to Fords of Avon

River Nethy

Strath Nethy

Coire Dearg

Bynack Beg

Bynack More
1090m

650

Cnap Coire na Spreidhe
1151m

Cairn Gorm

A Choinneach
1017m

700
700
800

1245m

900
850
800

The Saddle

1 km

N

850
800
750

Continued
↓Glen Avon 3↓

Loch Avon

River Avon

The Ryvoan Bothy

The track runs past the other side of the bothy – its red roof being visible from afar. Always open – please treat with respect.

Bynack Stable

The draughty shelter by the River Nethy footbridge. A replacement bridge was built June '89

Dorback Burn 1

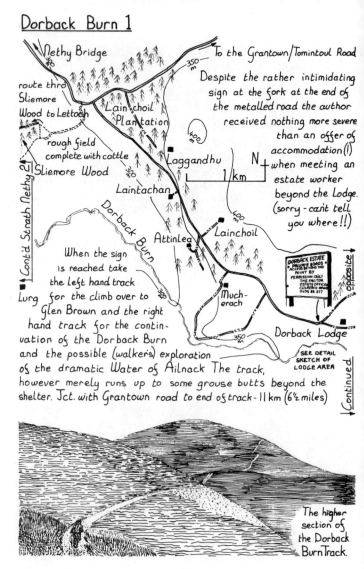

Nethy Bridge

To the Grantown/Tomintoul Road

route thro' Sliemore Wood to Lettoch

Lain'choil Plantation

rough field complete with cattle

Sliemore Wood

Laggandhu

1 km

N

Laintachan

Dorback Burn

Attinlea

Lainchoil

Cont'd Strath Nethy 21

Lurg

Mucherach

Dorback Lodge

DORBACK ESTATE PRIVATE ROADS ACCESS ROAD NO POINT BY PERMISSION ONLY ESTATE OFFICE CULREACH VIA 0479 88 277

SEE DETAIL SKETCH OF LODGE AREA

Despite the rather intimidating sign at the fork at the end of the metalled road the author received nothing more severe than an offer of accommodation (!) when meeting an estate worker beyond the Lodge. (sorry - can't tell you where !!)

When the sign is reached take the left hand track for the climb over to Glen Brown and the right hand track for the continuation of the Dorback Burn and the possible (walkers) exploration of the dramatic Water of Ailnack The track, however merely runs up to some grouse butts beyond the shelter. Jct. with Grantown road to end of track - 11 km (6½ miles)

The higher section of the Dorback Burn Track.

82

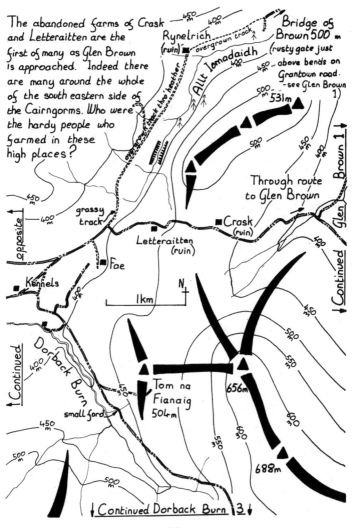

The abandoned farms of Crask and Letteraitten are the first of many as Glen Brown is approached. Indeed there are many around the whole of the south eastern side of the Cairngorms. Who were the hardy people who farmed in these high places?

Rynelrich (ruin)

overgrown track

Allt Iomadaidh

Bridge of Brown 500 m (rusty gate just above bends on Grantown road. — see Glen Brown 1)

overgrown track thro' heather

531m

Through route to Glen Brown

Glen Brown 1

grassy track

Crask (ruin)

Letteraitten (ruin)

opposite

Fae

Kennels

N

1km

Continued

Continued

Dorback Burn

small ford

Tom na Fianaig 504m

656m

688m

↓ Continued Dorback Burn 3 ↓

Dorback Burn 3

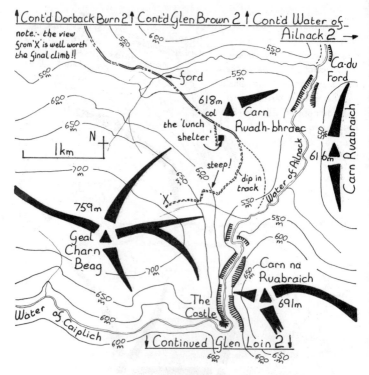

note:- the view from 'X' is well worth the final climb!!

ford

618m col

the 'lunch shelter'

Carn Ruadh-bhraec

Ca-du Ford

Carn Ruabraich

616m

N

1 km

steep!

dip in track

Water of Ailnack

'X'

759m

Geal Charn Beag

Carn na Ruabraich

691m

The Castle

Water of Caiplich

↓ Continued Glen Loin 2 ↓

This map repeats part of the Water of Ailnack map. No apologies however for illustrating this spectacular river gorge relative to the Dorback Burn. Though bikes have to be abandoned at 'X' the close proximity of the various routes comes as a surprise to those who explore the glens individually. Don't be fooled by the short distances as they appear on the map. The ground is rough and much of the gorge of the Water of Ailnack is either impassable to the ordinary walker or tough going for the intrepid explorer. There is a shelter but you're a long way from home!

The environs of Dorback Lodge

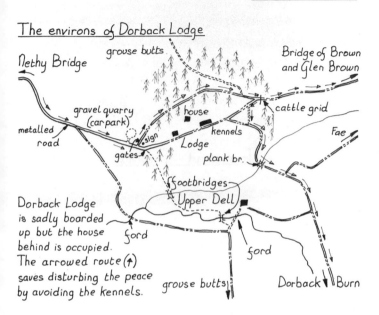

Nethy Bridge

grouse butts

Bridge of Brown
and Glen Brown

gravel quarry
(car park)

metalled
road

house

kennels

cattle grid

Fae

sign

Lodge

gates

plank br.

Footbridges

Upper Dell

Dorback Lodge
is sadly boarded
up but the house
behind is occupied.
The arrowed route (↑)
saves disturbing the peace
by avoiding the kennels.

ford

ford

grouse butts

Dorback Burn

The 'Lunch' Shelter

Tomintoul District

Tomintoul District

Access:- Access to Tomintoul from the south is via the notorious Lecht road - frequently blocked with snow in winter and rising to 640m. (My wife and I once had an epic tandem ride from Perth via the Cairnwell and the Lecht — 95 miles in a day, so this route has special memories for us). From the north the same road (A939) approaches from Grantown (and the A9). The east approach from Glen Livet is a route via the popular 'Whisky Trail'. The planned town of Tomintoul can appear bleak under a grey sky, lying on an exposed spur of high ground at 350m, however it still somehow retains a pioneering spirit and the warmth of its inhabitants compensates for its wild location. I like the place anyway

Accommodation:- Several hotels in Tomintoul, the odd B+B, and a simple Youth Hostel. Hotels also at Gairnshiel and Cock Br. Summer only tourist information in Tomintoul.

Geographical Features:- Most of the area surrounding the Rivers Avon and Gairn is bleak grouse moor divided by the spectacular Water of Ailnack gorge, Glen Avon, Glen Gairn and several lesser glens many of which are linked making through routes possible for walkers and cyclists. I have drawn the line at the A939 for the purposes of this book but many forest and farm tracks to the north and east are worthy of further exploration.

Mountains:- The great Glen Avon, or even better the Glen Gairn/Glen Builg/Glen Avon approach to the Cairngorm mountains is in my opinion unsurpassed. It is long, very long, amply supplied with bothies and shelter and the views into the mountains always spur you on. It is also a very committing route. Faindouran Lodge is about the remotest place in mainland Britain and any expedition into this area must be regarded as serious.

Even on a bike Tomintoul or Bridge of Gairn to
Faindouran and back is a very long day. Winter conditions
will rule out this area for many - remember a Cairngorm
blizzard can last four days and leave conditions
impassable in the 600m high glen. Having said all that Glen
Avon provides the finest access to Ben Avon, Beinn a
Bhuird and the true wilderness of Loch Avon and the
central area of the eastern Cairngorms.

Rivers:- The area is dominated by the Avon. Generally not
fordable, even at 'fords of Avon' despite the name! The
Avon is joined by the Burn of Loin, the Builg Burn and
Water of Ailnack on its way to Tomintoul and the Spey.
The River Gairn however turns south and joins the Dee. The
Don remains fiercely independent and makes its own way
to the sea just north of Aberdeen.

Forests:- Not much to offer apart from some plantations
above Glen Brown and south of Bridge of Brown. Some
fine if small birchwoods may be seen in the lower
reaches of Glen Avon.

Lochs:- The grandeur of Loch Avon has to be seen to be
fully realised. This place is the epitomy of all that is wild.
A truly sacred place for those who understand the need for
conserving such wilderness, indeed the very knowledge that the
other side of Cairn Gorm has been desecrated detracts
somehow from the feeling of true unspoilt wilderness that
even this place offers. Its splendid isolation has to be
defended to the last. Loch Builg is a pleasant sheet of
water sitting on the Gairn/Avon watershed.

Emergency:- There are public telephones in Tomintoul village;
at Gairnshiel (o.s. ref:- 293006); Dykehead telephone exchange
(o.s. ref:- 272087); and Bridge of Brown (o.s. ref:- 124206)
Shelters and bothies, and condition of same is noted on
the detail map pages.

Tomintoul District Routes 1

Glen Brown

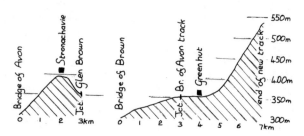

Water of Ailnack

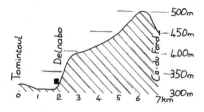

Glen Avon

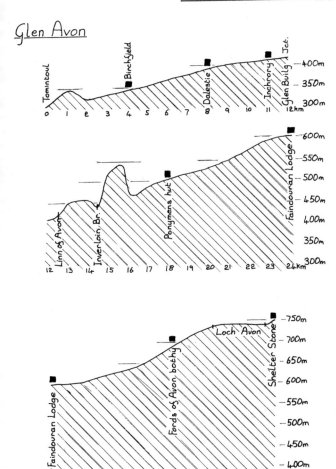

Tomintoul District Routes 3

Glen Loin

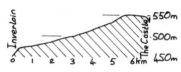

Strath Don

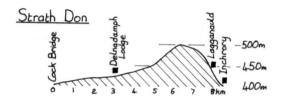

Glen Builg

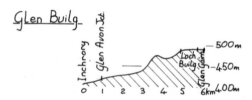

Glen Gairn

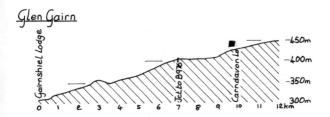

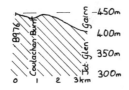

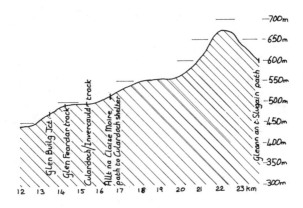

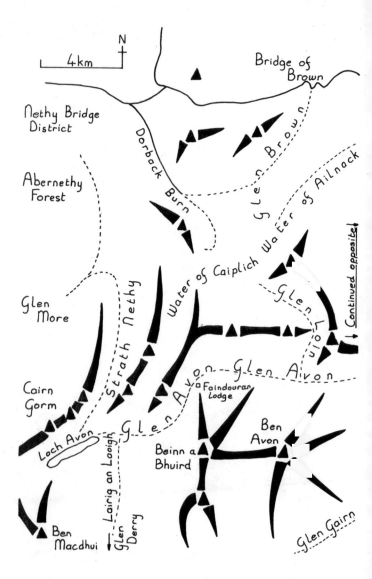

N

4km

Bridge of Brown

Nethy Bridge District

Glen Brown

Dorback Burn

Abernethy Forest

Water of Ailnack

Water of Caiplich

Glen More

Glen Loin

Strath Nethy

Continued opposite

Glen Avon

Glen Avon

Cairn Gorm

Faindouran Lodge

Glen Avon

Ben Avon

Loch Avon

Beinn a Bhuird

Lairig an Laoigh

Glen Derry

Ben Macdhui

Glen Gairn

94

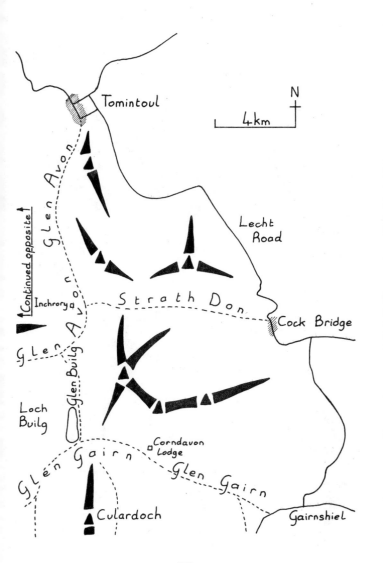

Tomintoul

N

4 km

Glen Avon

Continued opposite

Lecht Road

Inchrory

Strath Don

Cock Bridge

Glen Avon

Glen Buildg

Glen Avon

Loch Buildg

Glen Builg

Corndavon Lodge

Glen Gairn

Glen Gairn

Glén Gairn

Culardoch

Gairnshiel

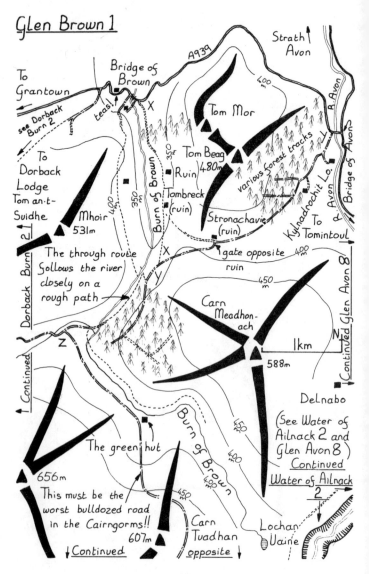

Glen Brown 1

Strath Avon ↑

A939

To Grantown

see Dorback Burn 2

Bridge of Brown

teas!

X

To Dorback Lodge

Tom an-t-Suidhe

Mhoir 531m

400

350

350

Burn of Brown

Tom Mor

600

Tom Beag 480m

Ruin

Tombreck (ruin)

various forest tracks

Stronachavie (ruin)

R. Avon

Bridge of Avon

Kylnadrochit Lo.

R. Avon

To Tomintoul

The through route follows the river closely on a rough path →

400

X

Y

gate opposite ruin

400 m

Carn Meadhon-ach

450 m

1km

N

588m

Dorback Burn 2 ←

← Continued

Z

Continued Glen Avon 8

Delnabo

(See Water of Ailnack 2 and Glen Avon 8)

Continued

Water of Ailnack 2

656m

The green hut

This must be the worst bulldozed road in the Cairngorms!!

450

Burn of Brown

400

607m

↓Continued

Carn Tuadhan opposite ↓

450

400

Lochan Uaine

96

Glen Brown may be approached (X-X) from Bridge of Brown by means of a track from the steep road 200m above the bridge which quickly degenerates into a path across the fields and derelict farms almost petering out before joining the forest road. The alternative start from Bridge of Avon (Y-Y) rises steeply above the beautiful Kylnadrochit Lodge to the ruined Stronachavie, then left through the gate. Where the routes X and Y join and before the forest is reached a zig-zag path leads down to a riverside path leading to the track from Dorback Lodge. A left turn is taken to the green hut and the diabolical scar that is the track beyond. The route west to east from Dorback Lodge to Bridge of Avon is a fine route linking Nethy Bridge and Tomintoul. At 'Z' turn left on a green track which becomes a path as the main track rises and continues to the green hut.

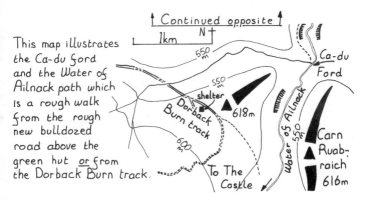

The green hut

This map illustrates the Ca-du ford and the Water of Ailnack path which is a rough walk from the rough new bulldozed road above the green hut or from the Dorback Burn track.

↑ Continued opposite ↑

1km   N

550m

550m

Ca-du Ford

shelter

Dorback Burn track

618m

Water of Ailnack

550

600m

To The Castle

Carn Ruab-raich

616m

Water of Ailnack 1

The Water of Ailnack gorge is a geographical feature completely out of character with the surrounding area. Across this drab expanse of grouse moor a dramatic gorge has been carved by the river through glacial moraine and rock creating an exciting prospect for exploration. Probably better explored on foot than with a mountainbike the gorge can easily be followed on its north west bank from Delnabo to the Ca-du ford. Glen Brown and the Dorback Burn track also provide walkers with access to the mid-section of the gorge. The Ca-du ford to The Castle section is mainly pathless and not as dramatic as the gorge below the ford, apart from The Castle itself which is best explored from the head of Glen Loin, an amazing feature in a bleak landscape. The river above The Castle is the Water of Caiplich which drains the remote area between the Abernethy Forest and Glen Avon, bounded to the west by Bynack More and the northern section of the Lairig an Laoigh route.

The Water of Ailnack

Delnabo

Burn of Brown

the green hut

track on ridge

400m

400

350

500

450

400

350

← Continued Glen Brown 1 and 2

The rough new Glen Brown track, not yet on O.S. maps - a dreadful scar.

Lochan Uaine

grassy shelf

450

500

450

550

450

400

350

800m link over pathless hill

498m

482m Tom an Reisg

600 m

450

550 m

Druimna h-Easgainn

N

1km

Allt Dearcaige

550 m

Ca du Ford

Carn Ruadh-bhreac 618m

← Continued Dorback Burn 3

lunch shelter

The Dorback Burn track

550

Water of Ailnack

Carn Ruabraich 616m

Allt Bheithachan

400

450

500

Continued Glen Avon 7 + 8 →

Carn an t-Sleibhe 589m

600 m

The Castle

600

650

Carn na Ruabraich 691m

600

Geal Charn 616m

↓ Continued Glen Loin 2 ↓

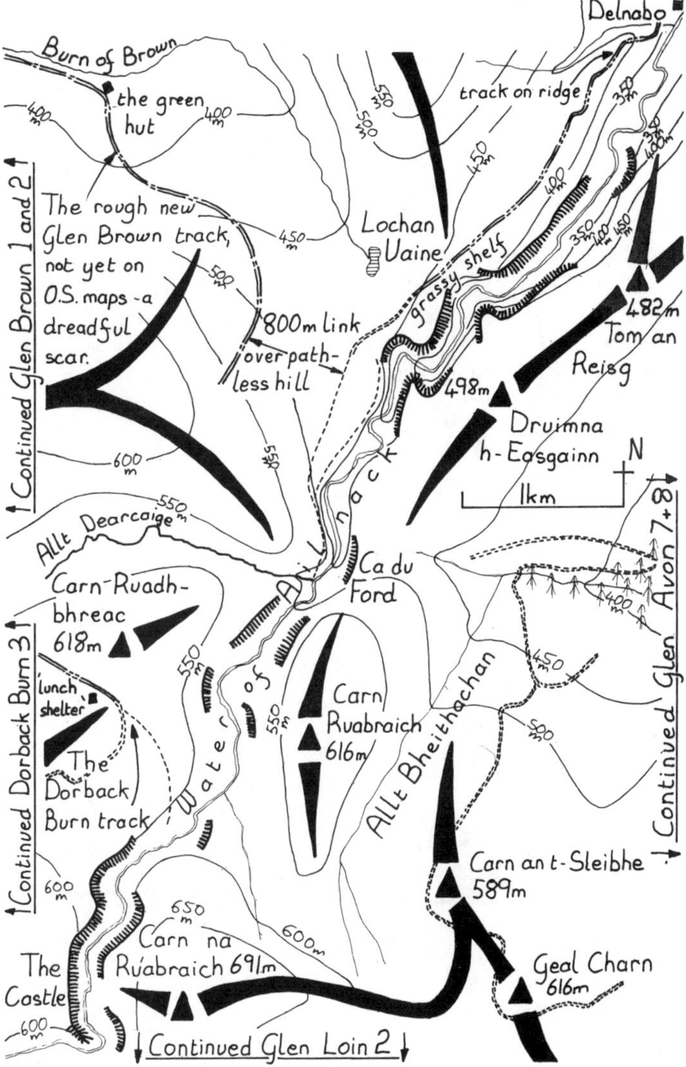

Glen Avon 1

Glen Avon starts in the magnificent setting of Loch Avon and continues east and north to the confluence of the Burn of Loin and the Builg Burn just below the Linn of Avon from which the Avon turns north. The upper reaches are well provided with bothies; The Shelter Stone 002016 being nothing more than a cave; the Fords of Avon Refuge being a wooden shed held down with rocks, difficult to find in snow; Faindouran Lo 082062 is a one roomed shelter with a fireplace (but nothing to burn!) and a low sleeping platform; The Ponymens Hut 129061 is a timber shed with seats, now no longer with a stove; the ruins above Inchrory at 181079 were demolished late in 1989. For safety reasons distances are set out in the tables below and due account should be taken relating to the weather forecast, fitness etc. Spare food, clothing and a sleeping bag should be taken into the upper reaches of the glen. Table of distances from Tomintoul:-

Inchrory	11 km	7 miles
Linn of Avon	12.5 km	8 miles
Inverloin	14 km	9 miles
The Ponymen's Hut	18 km	11.5 miles
Faindouran Lodge	24 km	15 miles
Fords of Avon	30 km	19 miles
The Shelter Stone	34 km	21.5 miles

Other distances are as follows from Linn of Avon:-

Loch Builg Boathouse	5 km	3 miles	
Corndavon Lodge	9 km	5.5 miles	
Cock Bridge	9 km	5.5 miles	via Strath Don
Gairnshiel	16 km	10 miles	via Corndavon Lo

The reward for covering all this distance is access to the central Cairngorm mountains which can be either just admired, or using the bothies for overnights can be walked and explored from the remote side. It is a rare privilege just to be in Glen Avon, to experience its unique remoteness and quiet and to savour that feeling of being so very far away from the 'rat race'. It is indeed a place to put life itself in perspective. Enough of this philosophy !! this is supposed to be a guidebook!

Note the Glen Avon maps start from the <u>head</u> of the glen

The Fords of Avon Bothy

The ruins just above Inchrory-demolished in late '89. They were on the right hand side of the track 100m along the Strath Don route east of Inchrory.

Glen Avon 3

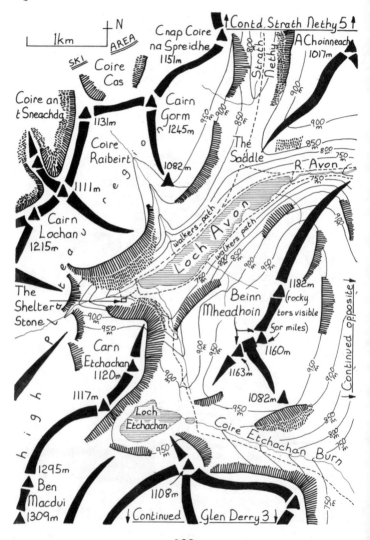

1km

N AREA

SKI

Coire Cas

Coire an t Sneachda

Cnap Coire na Spreidhe 1151m

↑ Contd. Strath Nethy 5 ↑

A Choinneach 1017m

Cairn Gorm 1245m

Strath Nethy

1131m

Coire Raibeirt

1082m

The Saddle

1111m

R. Avon

Cairn Lochan 1215m

walkers path

Loch Avon

walkers path

The Shelter Stone

1192m (rocky tors visible for miles)

Beinn Mheadhoin

1160m

Carn Etchachan 1120m

1163m

1082m

high

1117m

Loch Etchachan

Coire Etchachan Burn

← Continued opposite →

1295m

Ben Macdui 1309m

1108m

↓ Continued Glen Derry 3 ↓

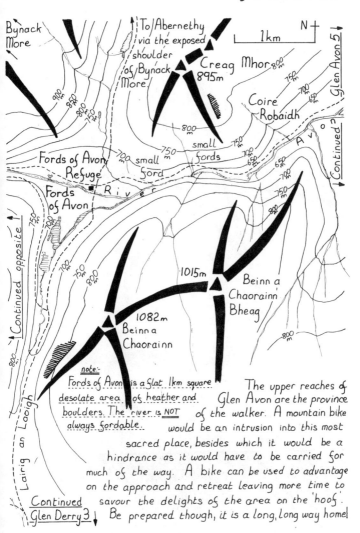

The upper reaches of Glen Avon are the province of the walker. A mountain bike would be an intrusion into this most sacred place, besides which it would be a hindrance as it would have to be carried for much of the way. A bike can be used to advantage on the approach and retreat leaving more time to savour the delights of the area on the 'hoof'. Be prepared though, it is a long, long way home!

Glen Avon 5

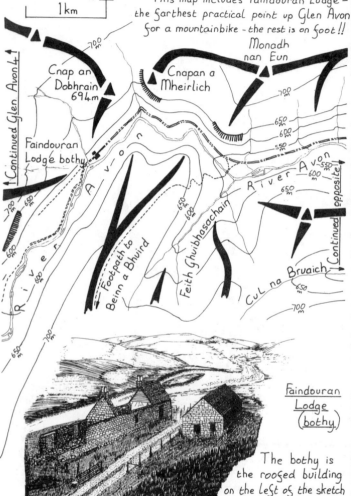

N

1 km

This map includes Faindouran Lodge – the farthest practical point up Glen Avon for a mountainbike – the rest is on foot!!

Continued Glen Avon 4

Cnap an Dobhrain 694m

700

Cnapan a Mheirlich

Monadh nan Eun

700
m

650
600
550

Faindouran Lodge bothy

R i v e r   A v o n

River Avon

600
550

Continued opposite

650

600

Footpath to Beinn a Bhuird

Feith Ghuibhasachain

Cul na Bruaich

650

650
m

R i v e r   A v o n

700
650

600

700

650

700

Faindouran Lodge (bothy.)

The bothy is the roofed building on the left of the sketch

104

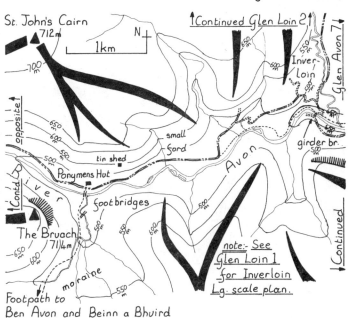

St. John's Cairn
712m

N

1km

↑Continued _Glen Loin 2_

Inver-
Loin

Glen Avon 7↑

700m

opposite↑

↑Contd.

650
600
500

tin shed ■

Ponymens Hut

small
ford

Avon

girder br.

River

footbridges

The Bruach
714m

650
600

550
600

550

600

note:- See
Glen Loin 1
for Inverloin
Lg. scale plan.

↓Continued

moraine

550

Footpath to
Ben Avon and Beinn a Bhuird

<u>The Ponymen's Hut</u>
<u>(bothy)</u>

"Erected for the
use of ponymen
on the Glen
Avon Estate."

Glen Avon 7

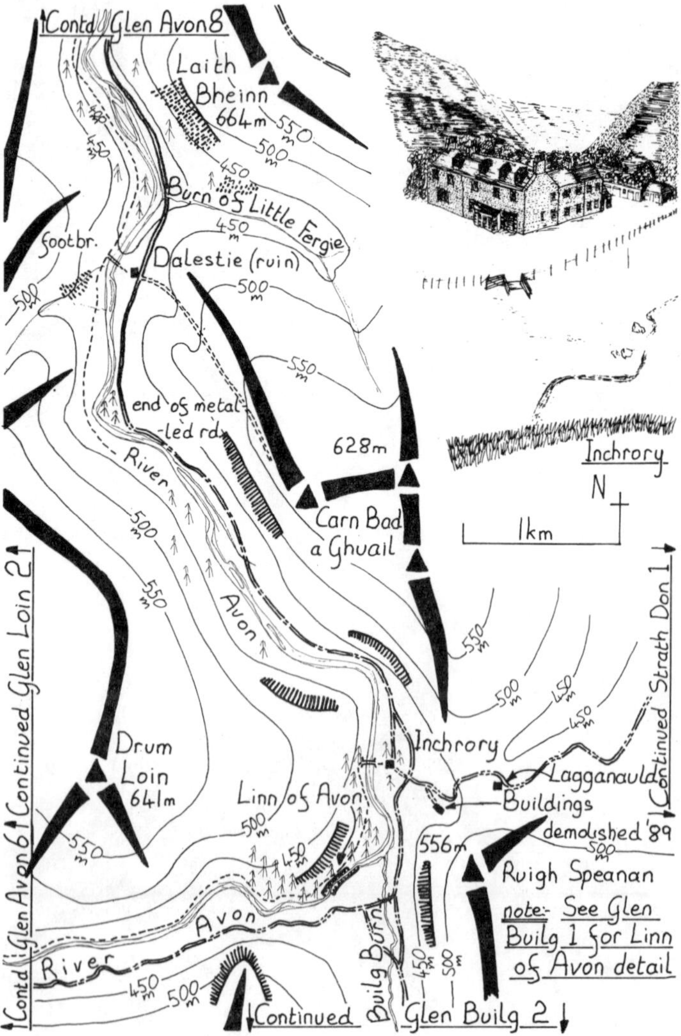

Contd Glen Avon 8
Laith Bheinn 664m
550 m
500 m
450 m
Burn of Little Fergie
footbr.
Dalestie (ruin)
end of metalled rd.
River
Avon
628m
Carn Bad a Ghuail
Inchrory
N
1km
Continued Glen Loin 2
Continued Strath Don 1
Drum Loin 641m
Inchrory
Lagganauld
Buildings demolished '89
Linn of Avon
556m
Ruigh Speanan
note:- See Glen Builg 1 for Linn of Avon detail
Contd Glen Avon 6
River Avon
Builg Burn
Continued Glen Builg 2

Any expedition into Glen Avon should start off with the short walk to the view indicator at Queens Cairn where the lower, green, reaches of the glen may be seen against a backdrop of the high tops. This view however relates not even a hint of the wildness of the upper reaches. The mood of the glen changes at the great bend at Linn of Avon 12·5km (8m) from Tomintoul, and again a mile or so beyond Faindouran bothy where the Land-rover track ends and the walkers path begins. Glen Avon has a great deal to offer.

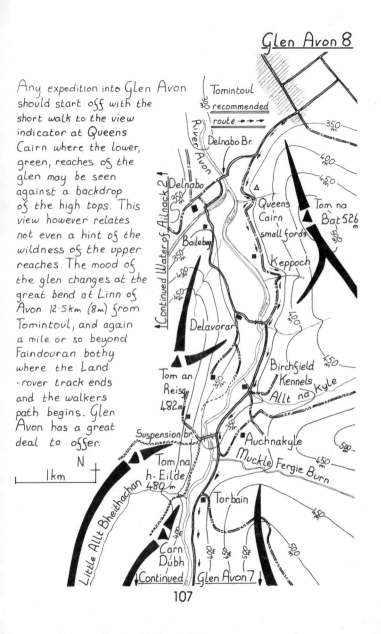

Tomintoul
recommended
route →→→

River Avon

Delnabo Br.

350m

350m

400m

450m

Delnabo

350m

←Continued Water of Ailnack 2

Bailebeg

350m

400m

450m

Queens Cairn

small fords

Tom na Bat 526m

500m

Keppoch

400m

Delavorar

450m

Tom an Reisg 482m

350m

Birchfield Kennels

Allt na Kyle

Suspension br.

Auchnakyle

Muckle Fergie Burn

500m

450m

350m

N
1km

Tom na h-Eilde 480m

Little Allt Bheithachan

Torbain

450m

400m

Carn Dubh

350m 400m 500m

500m

↓Continued Glen Avon 7↓

Glen Loin 1

Glen Loin has little to offer - it is a dull glen with drab heather clad hillsides and a good track. It provides the best access to view The Castle, a spectacular rocky gorge belonging to the Water of Ailnack but difficult to gain access from the north. A short walk across a low watershed suddenly brings the visitor to this spectacular piece of rock architecture conveniently placed to relieve one of the dull surroundings. At the other end of the glen Inverloin surely must have been the most remote spot in the Caingorms to run a farm. Now a ruin, a rough shelter provides for two (sitting up!) If needed the Burn of Loin may be difficult or even dangerous to cross and its probably not worth the effort. You'd never be found there - that's a certainty! The Castle is 7 km (4 miles) from Inverloin. Glen Loin makes a good side-trip on the way up or down Glen Avon if time (and fitness!) permit.

The environs of Inverloin

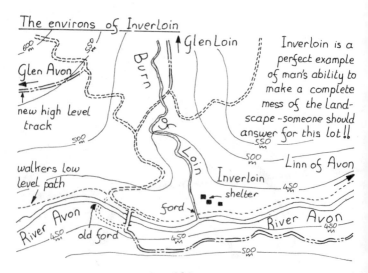

Inverloin is a perfect example of man's ability to make a complete mess of the landscape - someone should answer for this lot!!

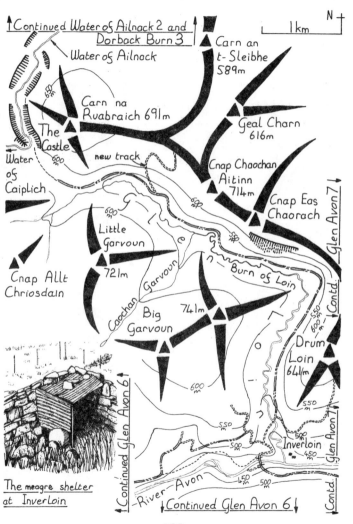

N

1 km

↑Continued Water of Ailnack 2 and
Dorback Burn 3 ↑

Water of Ailnack

Carn an
t-Sleibhe
589m

Carn na
Ruabraich 691m

Geal Charn
616m

The
Castle

Water
of
Caiplich

new track

Cnap Chaochan
Aitinn
714m

Cnap Eas
Chaorach

Little
Garvoun

721m

Glen Avon 7↑

Cnap Allt
Chriosdain

Burn of Loin

Caochan Garvoun

Big
Garvoun

741m

Drum
Loin
641m

Contd.

Inverloin

↓Continued Glen Avon 6↓

Continued Glen Avon 6↓

Glen Avon 7↓

Contd.

River Avon

The meagre shelter
at Inverloin

Strath Don 1

The River Don is only so named below Cock Bridge but this is the upper continuation of the Don to the Feith Bhait/Glen Avon watershed. The road is unfortunately metalled part of the way above Cock Bridge and there is little ascent making this a very easy route. Inchrory to Cock Br - 9km.

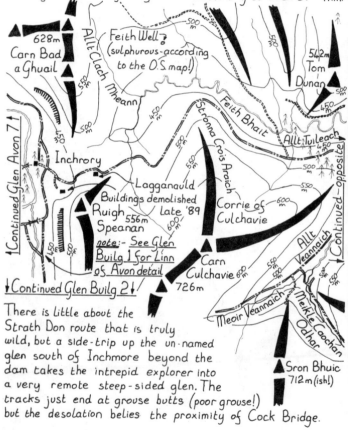

628m
Carn Bad
a Ghuail

Allt Clach Mheann

Feith Well
(sulphurous-according
to the O.S. map!)

500 m

542m
Tom
Dunan

450 m

550

450

500

Feith Bhait

Allt Tuileach

450
500 m

Inchrory

Stronna Crois Aroich

Corrie of
Culchavie

600

550

550

Continued – opposite

Lagganauld
Buildings demolished
late '89

Ruigh 556m
Speanan

600

Allt Veannaich

500 550

note:- See Glen
Builg 1 for Linn
of Avon detail

↓Continued Glen Builg 2↓

←Continued Glen Avon 7↑

450

500

Carn
Culchavie
726m

600

500

Meoir Veannaich

Meikle Caochan Odhar

Sron Bhuic
712m (ish!)

There is little about the Strath Don route that is truly wild, but a side-trip up the un-named glen south of Inchmore beyond the dam takes the intrepid explorer into a very remote steep-sided glen. The tracks just end at grouse butts (poor grouse!) but the desolation belies the proximity of Cock Bridge.

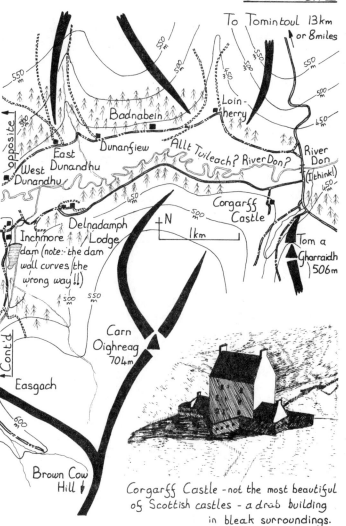

To Tomintoul 13km
or 8miles

550m

Badnabein

Loin-
herry

opposite

East
Dunandhu

Dunanfiew

Allt Tuileach? River Don?

River
Don
(I think!)

West
Dunandhu

450m

Corgarff
Castle

Delnadamph
Lodge

N

500m

1km

Inchmore
dam (note:- the dam
wall curves the
wrong way!!)

Tom a
Gharraidh
506m

Cont'd

500m   550m

Carn
Oighreag
704m

Easgach

600m

Brown Cow
Hill

Corgarff Castle - not the most beautiful
of Scottish castles - a drab building
in bleak surroundings.

111

Glen Builg 1

Glen Builg (pron. Bulig) provides an important link from Glen Avon/ Glen Loin/ Strath Don to Glen Gairn which, via the Culardoch cols links Tomintoul with Braemar - virtually all "off-road" a paradise for the mountainbiker and providing some fine long marches for the walker. The area is well provided with bothies, the boathouse had a new floor/sleeping platform in May '90 and Corndavon Lodge in Glen Gairn has to be the best bothy in the area - if a little too accessible ie-busy! Glen Builg reminds one of the English Lakeland scenery as the track winds its way 5km (3 miles) from Linn of Avon to the Glen Gairn track at the flat watershed south of Loch Builg among the Lochans. Arctic char, left by the last ice age reside in the loch - also eels which are fished every few years providing a high quality catch from the pollution free Loch.

Loch Builg.
Boathouse
(bothy).

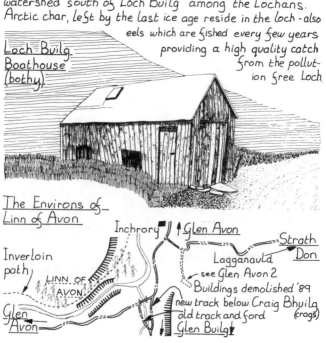

The Environs of
Linn of Avon

Inchrory
↑ Glen Avon

Inverloin
path

LINN OF
AVON

Strath
Don

Lagganauld
see Glen Avon 2
Buildings demolished '89
new track below Craig Bhuilg
old track and ford
Glen Builg↓ (crags)

Glen
Avon

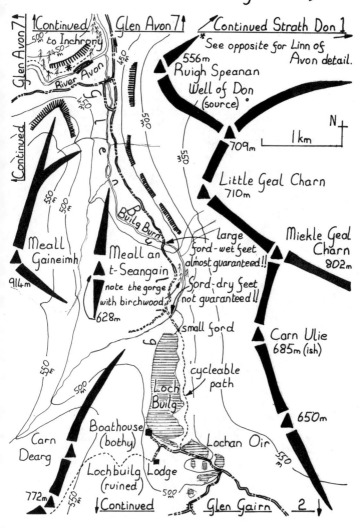

Continued Strath Don 1

* See opposite for Linn of Avon detail.

Continued to Inchrory

Glen Avon 7

Glen Avon 7

500m

750 / 50m

River Avon

650

500

550

500

Continued

550

500

Builg Burn

500

556m
Ruigh Speanan

Well of Don
(source)

709m

N

1 km

Little Geal Charn
710m

Miekle Geal Charn
802m

Meall Gaineimh

914m

Meall an t-Seangain

note the gorge with birchwood

628m

large ford - wet feet almost guaranteed!!

ford - dry feet not guaranteed!!

small ford

cycleable path

550

500

Loch Builg

Carn Ulie
685m (ish)

650m

550

Carn Dearg

Boathouse (bothy)

Lochan Oir

Lochbuilg Lodge (ruined)

500

Glen Gairn   2

772m

550

Continued

Glen Gairn 1

Glen Gairn has a good track all the way to Loch Builg via the excellent Corndavon Lodge bothy. From Loch Builg one has a choice of route:- down Glen Builg to Glen Avon and thence to Tomintoul or Faindouran/Loch Avon; the walkers path through to Gleann an t-Slugain; the climb over the Culardoch col to Invercauld and Braemar.
The Glen Gairn/Glen Builg/Glen Avon route to the Shelter Stone has to be the longest and most satisfying approach route to the mountains anywhere in Britain.

Carn Dearg

Continued opposite

Stuc Gharbh Mhor
1115m approx.

743m

Carn Drochaid

1km N

note:- the fords are very fast flowing in flood!!

Clachdhu

600 m   550 m

br.

Sord

Sord

Sord

River Gairn

550 m

600

Creag an Dail Bheag

862m

Culardoch shelter

Carn Liath

862m

Continued Gleann an t-Slugain 3

Continued Gleann an t-Slugain 2 and 4

114

Loch Builg

Boathouse

↑ Continued Glen Builg 2 ↑

Lochan Oir

Lochbuilg Lo (ruin)

Corndavon Lo.

bothy

footbr. + ford

550

500

450

ruin

X   X

River Gairn

450

500

footbridge and ford

500

Culardoch Beag

550

opposite ↑

← Continued

Continued Glen Gairn 3

Continued Glen

note:- the ruined shielings at X

note:- the mural in the only maintained room in the Lodge. This room was used by the Queen Mother's hunting parties. Such a pity the Royal Family have to go around shooting/killing foxes etc.

Tom Breac

N

1km

Continued Glen Feardar 1 ↓

Culardoch 900m ▲

← Continued Gleann an t-Slugain 2 and 4

The bothy, near Corndavon Lodge

Glen Gairn 3

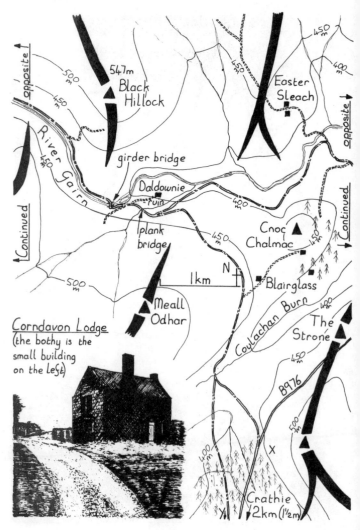

547m
Black Hillock

500 m

450

450

opposite ↑

450

450

450

400

Easter Sleach

River Gairn

girder bridge

Daldownie
ruin

400 m

Continued ←

opposite →

plank bridge

450

Cnoc Chalmac

450

Blairglass

Continued →

1km

N

500 m

Meall Odhar

Coylachan Burn

450

400

The Strone

Corndavon Lodge
(the bothy is the small building on the left)

B976

500

400 m

×

Crathie
2km (1½m)

657m

N

1km

A939

450m

450m

Shenval

450m

400m

Torran

Loinahaun

GLEN GAIRN

R. Tomnavey

River Gairn

A939

350m

Gairnshiel Lo

opposite

Continued

R. Gairn

350m

350m

400m

450m

Rineten

Braenaloin

B976

start from Braenaloin
to follow the river Gairn all the
way. Alternatively start from point X
on the Crathie road or 1·5 km south at Y
just off the edge of the page (sorry!) via the forest
road - all of which link up with the main Glen Gairn

track before the girder bridge is reached.

X to Carndavon = 7 km (4 miles)
Y to Carndavon = 8·5 km (5 miles)
Braenaloin to Carndavon = 7 km (4 miles)
Carndavon to Loch Builg = 4·5 km (3 miles)

The girder
bridge

Link Routes and the Cairngorm Circuit

The following 'link routes' are suggested through routes between the main centres around the Cairngorm Mountains. Useful as a quick reference guide showing alternatives where possible and with indication of connections to other glens which are the subject of chapters in this book.

The link routes are quite committing if undertaken in a day, forming either long distance walks or a full day out on a mountainbike. These routes are serious in winter and equipment and fitness should reflect this.

It becomes obvious that a complete 'Cairngorm Circuit' is possible almost entirely off-road covering a distance of roughly 132km or 82miles. This is ideal for a weeks holiday, the mountainbiker having more scope for exploring other glens as side-trips than the walker.

Accommodation may be tent/bothy/hostel/B+B or 3 star hotel to choice, all of which are liberally but not obtrusively situated at convenient locations around the route.

This Circuit is indeed the very basis for exploration of the glens as the starting point for every route is passed on its winding route around this great plateau.

The high mountain passes of the Lairig Ghru and Lairig an Laoigh are omitted as to describe these as mere glens is an understatement and they are certainly not in the author's opinion a bike ride! though many have crossed both with (not on!) a bike, which is about as much use as a bedstead over these routes! They can of course be walked, but much has been written elsewhere. Their inclusion would be repetitious.

Note:-

These, then, are the limitations of this book in terms of both height (because it is not a mountaineer's guide) and area (apart from Glen Ey the 'Circuit' is the border). However the author hopes that these deliberate limitations are more than compensated by the detail possible in the small area chosen rather than attempting the whole of Scotland at one go.

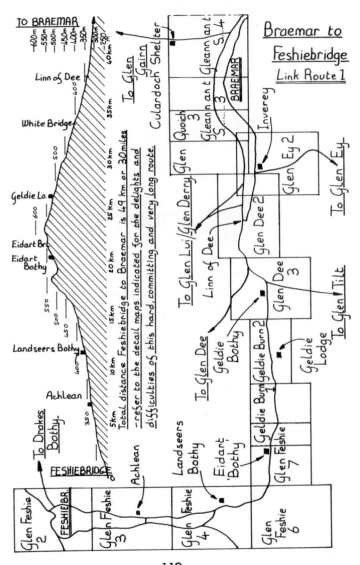

Braemar to Feshiebridge
Link Route 1

TO BRAEMAR

-600m
-550m
-500m
-450m
-400m
-350m
-300m
-250m

40km
45km
400
500
600
550
500
450
400
350

Linn of Dee
White Bridge
Geldie La.
Eidart Br.
Eidart Bothy
Landseers Bothy
Achlean
FESHIEBRIDGE

0   5km   10km   15km   20km   25km   30km   35km

Total distance Feshiebridge to Braemar is 49 km or 30 miles – refer to the detail maps indicated for the delights and difficulties of this hard committing and very long route.

To Glen Gairn   Culardoch Shelter
To Glen Quoich   Gleann an t Slugain 3   BRAEMAR   Gleann an t S. 4
Inverey
To Glen Lui/Glen Derry/Glen   Glen Ey 2   To Glen Ey
Linn of Dee   Glen Dee 2
To Glen Dee   Glen Dee 3   To Glen Tilt
Geldie Bothy   Geldie Lodge
Geldie Burn 2   To Glen Tilt
Eidart Bothy   Geldie Burn 1
Landseers Bothy   Glen Feshie 7
Achlean   Glen Feshie 6
To Drakes Bothy.
Glen Feshie 2   FESHIEBR.   Glen Feshie 3   Glen Feshie 4

119

NETHY BRIDGE

300m

30km

25km

To the Dorback Burn

Strath Nethy 4

Total distance Feshiebridge to Nethy Bridge is 30 km or 19 miles. refer to detail maps for the many variations possible on this easy route via forest and lochside. Look out for those high gates around Loch an Eilein and Loch Morlich !!

To Glen Avon

NETHY BR.

Strath Nethy 2

Strath Nethy 3

Strath Nethy 5

To Loch Avon

400m — 350m — 300m — 250m — 200m

25km

Glen More

Ryvoan Bothy

Loch Morlich

Milton Burn

Glen Einich 1

To Gleann Einich

Ryvoan Bothy

20km

400m

Loch Morlich

15km

350m

Glen Einich 1

Loch an Eilein 2

Loch an Eilein

To Gleann Einich

Cairngorm Club footbr.

10km

300m

Drakes Bothy 2

Loch an Eilein

5km

Drakes Bothy

Glen Feshie 2

FESHIE BRIDGE

Drakes Bothy

Glen Feshie 2

To Glen Feshie

FESHIEBRIDGE

0

Nethy Bridge to Tomintoul
Link Route 3

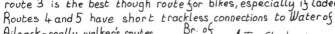

Total distance
Nethy Bridge to
Tomintoul is 21 km
or 13 miles approx.
_Choose your route
carefully !!_

Note:-

There are five options between Dorback Lodge and Tomintoul.
1. Via Rynelrich to Bridge of Brown.
2. Via lower Glen Brown to Bridge of Brown.
3. Via Stronachavie to Bridge of Avon. (see 'profile' above)
4. Via the 'green hut' and Water of Ailnack.
5. Via the upper Dorback Burn and Water of Ailnack.
Routes 1 and 2 involve short rough sections for mountainbikers,
route 3 is the best though route for bikes, especially if laden.
Routes 4 and 5 have short trackless connections to Water of
Ailnack - really walker's routes.

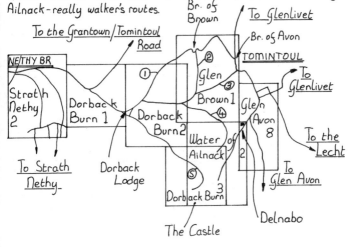

121

Tomintoul to Braemar
Link Route 4

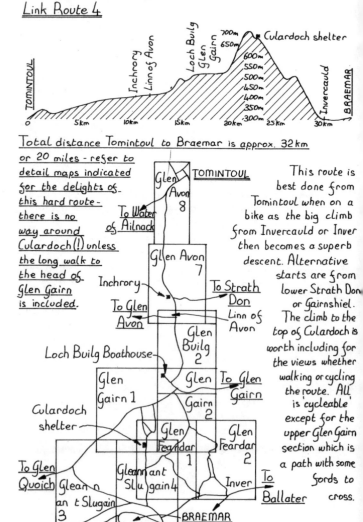

Total distance Tomintoul to Braemar is approx. 32km
or 20 miles - refer to detail maps indicated for the delights of this hard route - there is no way around Culardoch (!) unless the long walk to the head of Glen Gairn is included.

This route is best done from Tomintoul when on a bike as the big climb from Invercauld or Inver then becomes a superb descent. Alternative starts are from lower Strath Don or Gairnshiel. The climb to the top of Culardoch is worth including for the views whether walking or cycling the route. All is 'cycleable' except for the upper Glen Gairn section which is a path with some fords to cross.

Well that's it. It's just about finished. Two years of 'research' in the Cairngorms cycling and walking every inch (sorry, every centimetre) of track, taking countless record photographs, many winter evenings writing, mapping and sketching. I've never done any sketching before - hope it's OK. Seems a bit of an anti-climax. Perhaps I'll write another book - there is so much to 'go at' in Scotland, where next? It would have to be wild - probably in the west. First though a willing publisher must be found so we will then have to consider the future. I do hope the sensible, responsible element in mountainbiking wins over the growing "idiot" element. A good national club may help. I must not forget the walker. I walked the mountains for years before taking up mountainbiking - and still do. I can't get used to the "funny looks" (as if I shouldn't be there) I get from walkers when I'm cycling - they don't look like that when I'm walking! A bit of tolerance is needed. I also road cycle - solo and tandem. For me mountainbiking fills the gap between walkers' paths and roads. A safe haven for the cyclist - great with children away from the traffic. Bikes don't belong on the mountain tops - this is the province of the walker. Nor do mountain bikes belong on the road - they are too slow! The tracks make good long distance walks - another "weakness" of mine; as approaches, on foot (or by bike), for a few days in the wild, climbing and walking the high tops. These excursions into the wild keep me sane (I think so anyway!) away from the hassle of urban life and all that - I hope it does the same for you.

———————— ‖ ————————

CICERONE GUIDES

Cicerone publish a wide range of reliable guides to walking and climbing in Europe

FRANCE
TOUR OF MONT BLANC
CHAMONIX MONT BLANC - A Walking Guide
TOUR OF THE OISANS: GR54
WALKING THE FRENCH ALPS: GR5
THE CORSICAN HIGH LEVEL ROUTE: GR20
THE WAY OF ST JAMES: GR65
THE PYRENEAN TRAIL: GR10
TOUR OF THE QUEYRAS
ROCK CLIMBS IN THE VERDON

FRANCE / SPAIN
WALKS AND CLIMBS IN THE PYRENEES
ROCK CLIMBS IN THE PYRENEES

SPAIN
WALKS & CLIMBS IN THE PICOS DE EUROPA
WALKING IN MALLORCA
BIRDWATCHING IN MALLORCA
COSTA BLANCA CLIMBS

FRANCE / SWITZERLAND
THE JURA - Walking the High Route and Winter Ski Traverses
CHAMONIX TO ZERMATT The Walker's Haute Route

SWITZERLAND
WALKS IN THE ENGADINE
THE VALAIS - A Walking Guide
THE ALPINE PASS ROUTE

GERMANY / AUSTRIA
THE KALKALPEN TRAVERSE
KLETTERSTEIG - Scrambles
WALKING IN THE BLACK FOREST
MOUNTAIN WALKING IN AUSTRIA
WALKING IN THE SALZKAMMERGUT
KING LUDWIG WAY

ITALY
ALTA VIA - High Level Walkis in the Dolomites
VIA FERRATA - Scrambles in the Dolomites
ITALIAN ROCK - Selected Rock Climbs in Northern Italy
CLASSIC CLIMBS IN THE DOLOMITES
WALKING IN THE DOLOMITES

OTHER AREAS
THE MOUNTAINS OF GREECE - A Walker's Guide
CRETE: Off the beaten track
Treks & Climbs in the mountains of RHUM & PETRA, JORDAN
THE ATLAS MOUNTAINS

GENERAL OUTDOOR BOOKS
LANDSCAPE PHOTOGRAPHY
FIRST AID FOR HILLWALKERS
MOUNTAIN WEATHER
MOUNTAINEERING LITERATURE
THE ADVENTURE ALTERNATIVE

CANOEING
SNOWDONIA WILD WATER, SEA & SURF
WILDWATER CANOEING
CANOEIST'S GUIDE TO THE NORTH EAST

CARTOON BOOKS
ON FOOT & FINGER
ON MORE FEET & FINGERS
LAUGHS ALONG THE PENNINE WAY

 CICERONE PRESS

Also a full range of guidebooks to walking, scrambling, ice-climbing, rock climbing, and other adventurous pursuits in Britain and abroad

Other guides are constantly being added to the Cicerone List.
Available from bookshops, outdoor equipment shops or direct (send for price list)
from CICERONE, 2 POLICE SQUARE, MILNTHORPE, CUMBRIA, LA7 7PY

CICERONE GUIDES

Cicerone publish a wide range of reliable guides to walking and climbing in Britain - and other general interest books

LAKE DISTRICT - General Books
LAKELAND VILLAGES
WORDSWORTH'S DUDDON REVISITED
THE REGATTA MEN
REFLECTIONS ON THE LAKES
OUR CUMBRIA
PETTIE
THE HIGH FELLS OF LAKELAND
CONISTON COPPER A History
LAKELAND - A taste to remember (Recipes)
THE LOST RESORT?
CHRONICLES OF MILNTHORPE
LOST LANCASHIRE

LAKE DISTRICT - Guide Books
CASTLES IN CUMBRIA
WESTMORLAND HERITAGE WALK
IN SEARCH OF WESTMORLAND
CONISTON COPPER MINES
SCRAMBLES IN THE LAKE DISTRICT
MORE SCRAMBLES IN THE LAKE DISTRICT
WINTER CLIMBS IN THE LAKE DISTRICT
WALKS IN SILVERDALE/ARNSIDE
BIRDS OF MORECAMBE BAY
THE EDEN WAY

NORTHERN ENGLAND (outside the Lakes
THE YORKSHIRE DALES A walker's guide
WALKING IN THE SOUTH PENNINES
LAUGHS ALONG THE PENNINE WAY
WALKS IN THE YORKSHIRE DALES (3 VOL)
WALKS TO YORKSHIRE WATERFALLS
NORTH YORK MOORS Walks
THE CLEVELAND WAY & MISSING LINK
DOUGLAS VALLEY WAY
THE RIBBLE WAY
WALKING NORTHERN RAILWAYS EAST
WALKING NORTHERN RAILWAYS WEST
HERITAGE TRAILS IN NW ENGLAND
BIRDWATCHING ON MERSEYSIDE
THE LANCASTER CANAL
FIELD EXCURSIONS IN NW ENGLAND
ROCK CLIMBS LANCASHIRE & NW
THE ISLE OF MAN COASTAL PATH

DERBYSHIRE & EAST MIDLANDS
WHITE PEAK WALKS - 2 Vols
HIGH PEAK WALKS
WHITE PEAK WAY
KINDER LOG
THE VIKING WAY
THE DEVIL'S MILL (Novel)
WHISTLING CLOUGH (Novel)
WALES & WEST MIDLANDS
THE RIDGES OF SNOWDONIA
HILLWALKING IN SNOWDONIA
ASCENT OF SNOWDON
WELSH WINTER CLIMBS
SNOWDONIA WHITE WATER SEA & SURF
SCRAMBLES IN SNOWDONIA
ROCK CLIMBS IN WEST MIDLANDS
THE SHROPSHIRE HILLS A Walker's Guide
SOUTH & SOUTH WEST ENGLAND
WALKS IN KENT
THE WEALDWAY & VANGUARD WAY
SOUTH DOWNS WAY & DOWNS LINK
COTSWOLD WAY
WALKING ON DARTMOOR
SOUTH WEST WAY - 2 Vol
SCOTLAND
SCRAMBLES IN LOCHABER
SCRAMBLES IN SKYE
THE ISLAND OF RHUM
CAIRNGORMS WINTER CLIMBS
WINTER CLIMBS BEN NEVIS & GLENCOE
SCOTTISH RAILWAY WALKS
TORRIDON A Walker's Guide
SKI TOURING IN SCOTLAND

> THE MOUNTAINS OF ENGLAND & WALES
> VOL 1 WALES
> VOL 2 ENGLAND

Also a full range of guidebooks to walking, scrambling, ice-climbing, rock climbing, and other adventurous pursuits in Europe

Other guides are constantly being added to the Cicerone List.
Available from bookshops, outdoor equipment shops or direct (send for price list)
from CICERONE, 2 POLICE SQUARE, MILNTHORPE, CUMBRIA, LA7 7PY

Printed in Gt. Britain by
CARNMOR PRINT & DESIGN
95-97 LONDON RD. PRESTON